ANNIE JOHNSON FLINT

Grace Sufficient

One Hundred Further Poems by Annie Johnson Flint

HAYDEN PRESS
PUBLISHING

Contents

Preface

Welcome to the third volume of poems by Annie Johnson Flint in this collection. We trust that you will find as much comfort, encouragement and joy in them as countless thousands of people have done in the generations before us. If you do, then you will be interested to know that we have recently published other material concerning Annie, in both paperback and eBook formats.

Of course, there are the first two volumes in this series. "He Giveth More Grace" is the first volume of 100 poems, and the title poem is probably her most well-known. This volume also contains an abridged version of the biography of Annie by Roland V. Bingham. (If you would like to read the unabridged version, then you will find this in our "The Making of the Beautiful - The Life Story of Annie Johnson Flint." Both the full biography and the 100 poems from the first volume are contained in our "Annie Johnson Flint Compendium", which is particularly useful as a gift to introduce Annie to yet more readers. What we have found is that lovers of Annie's work just cannot wait to share it with others!) The second volume of poems - "Grace Sufficient" - rounds off the collection. You can find descriptions and links to the standalone publications at the end of the book.

We are also very excited to let you know about our audiobook of "He Giveth More Grace" with fabulous narration from the Los Angeles actor Abigail Reno. This is now available from all the major online audiobook stores, as well as local libraries for borrowing. We also anticipate producing audiobooks for the remaining material in the near future, so please do look out for them! If you would like to listen to a short sample, you can find it on Soundcloud, or click on this link.

Finally, if you would like to participate in an online community that celebrates the work of Annie Johnson Flint, and get the opportunity for free Annie-related downloads, then you might wish to follow the The Poetry of Annie Johnson Flint Facebook page: https://www.facebook.com/anniejohnsonflint.

GRACE SUFFICIENT

So many burdened lives along the way!
My load seems lighter than the most I see,
And oft I wonder if I could be brave,
Patient and sweet if they were laid on me.
But God has never said that He would give
Another's grace without another's thorn;
What matter, since for every day of mine
Sufficient grace for me comes with the morn?
And though the future brings some heavier cross
I need not cloud the present with my fears;
I know the grace that is enough today
Will be sufficient still through all the years.[1] [2]

---

[1] And he said unto me, My grace is sufficient for thee: for my strength is made perfect in weakness. Most gladly therefore will I rather glory in my infirmities, that the power of Christ may rest upon me. (2 Corinthians 12:9)

[2] The Lord is my strength and my shield; my heart trusted in him, and I am helped: therefore my heart greatly rejoiceth; and with my song will I praise him. (Psalm 28:7)

THE ANCHORED WILL

As on the surface of the sea
The little ripples run,
And all the foamy, twinkling waves
Are glinting in the sun,
So on the surface of my life
Drifts many a shining thought,
And moods and wishes and desires
In changing currents caught.
As ships in harbor swing and sway
With every turning tide,
Yet in the bedded rocks below
The holding anchors bide,
So, though my purpose seems to veer
Unstable as the sea,
And strain against the Hand that holds,
And struggles to be free,
Yet in my being's ocean depths
The restless waves are still,
And there my will is anchored fast
To God's unchanging will.

JUST FOR THEE

Not for peace and not for power,
Not for joy and not for light,
Not for truth and not for knowledge,
Not for courage in the flight,
Not for the strength to do Thee service -
Not for these my prayer shall be;
Not for any gifts or graces,
But for Thee, Lord, just for Thee.

Make me lonely for Thy presence
Every earthly friend above,
Make me thirst for Thine indwelling,
Make me hungry for Thy love,
Till in full and free surrender
I shall yield my life to Thee;
Only then, in full perfection
Canst Thou give Thyself to me.

All the beauty that I seek for,
Every treasure I would own,
Thou art these in rich completeness,
They are found in Thee alone;
All the loveliness I long for,
All the best that I would be,

I can never find them elsewhere
Than in Thee, Lord, just in Thee.

Empty me of all my glory,
All my boasting, all my pride;
Let my righteousness, my wisdom,
On Thy cross be crucified;
Fill me then with all Thy fulness,
All Thy will work Thou for me;
In Thyself in nothing lacking,
Make me, Lord, complete in Thee.[3]

---

[3] In Him dwelleth all the fulness of the Godhead ... and ye are complete in Him. (Colossians 2:9,10)

MY WINGS

"I cannot walk, but I can fly,"
No roof can house me from the stars,
No dwelling pen me in its bounds,
Nor keep me fast with locks and bars;
No narrow room my thoughts can cage,
No fetters hold my roving mind;
From these four walls that shut me in
My soaring soul a way can find.

With books and pictures at my side
All lands, all ages, are my own;
I dwell among the master minds,
The best and greatest earth has known;
I flee to strange and storied scenes
Of long ago and far away,
And roam where saints and heroes trod
In time's forgotten Yesterday.

With every wandering butterfly
Or singing bird on vagrant wing
My fancy takes the airy trail,
And follow it, adventuring,
Till higher than their highest flight,
Where cloud-ships drift and star-beams shine,

I rise on tireless pinions fleet,
And all the realms of space are mine.

From out the paling sunset skies
The Twilight Angel comes to me
On dusky wings to bear me swift
To shadowy haunts of Memory
Where, 'mid the gardens and the graves,
I wander, smiling through my tears,
With all the dear and deathless dead,
The loved and lost of vanished years.

And, when the long, long day is done,
I clasp the dearest Book of all
And through the dim, sweet silences
I hear my Father's accents fall;
Then, though in chains, yet am I free,
Beyond the pressure of my care,
Above earth's night my spirit mounts
On eagle wings of faith and prayer.

THINE WE ARE

"Thine are we" what joy , what comfort
This assurance brings the hearts!
Thine by purchase and redemption,
Nevermore from Thee to part;
By the Father's grace and pardon,
By Thy precious blood outpoured,
By the power that protects us
With the spirit's two edged sword;
Thine by our own full surrender,
Thine for service glad and free;
For Thy love our love has kindled,
And our souls are knit to Thee.

"On Thy side" - what peace, what safety!
Thou art Conqueror and King,
We shall follow Thee in triumph,
And Thy victory shall sing;
Undismayed and undefeated,
Prince of peace, oh, lead us on,
To thy kingdom and thy glory
When the final strife is won.
Sure defence in camp and conflict,
Great Commander, lead and guide.

"Thine are we" - what joy, what comfort!
Oh, what safety! "on Thy side."

BE YE ALSO READY

"What are the signs of Thy coming,
And when shall the end-time be?"
Anxious, they questioned the Master,
Curious, even as we.
Are these the signs of His coming
That loom over sea and land,
That darken the earth and the heavens?
Is the day so near at hand?
We know not; He hath not told us
This secret of the Lord,
But all we need He hath left us
To read in His sacred word.
And pulsing through the silence
Like the far, faint throb of a drum;
"Watch, be ye also ready,
For ye know not when I come."
Sweet as a silver trumpet
Through tumult and clamor clear;
"Watch, be ye also ready.
For the time is drawing near."[4]

---

[4] What shall be the sign of thy coming and of the end of the age? ... Be ye also ready. (Matthew
24:3,44)

BEHOLD, I COME

"Behold, I come," His voice is calling
    Above the conflicts of the world,
Above the crash of high thrones falling
    Above earthly empires downward hurled;
Above the tramp of armies treading,
    The bugles' blare, the cannon's roar,
Above the flames of strife, still spreading
    As host on host goes forth to war.

"Behold, I come," His voice is crying,
    Above the voices of the earth,
Above the shouting and the sighing,
    Above the moaning and the mirth;
Above the mandates of the monarchs,
    The impious prayers their lips have said,
Above the mourning of the mothers,
    Above the children's cries for bread.

"Behold, I come"; ye people, hear Him,
    The day of man is well-nigh spent;
Above your heads the skies will darken,
    Beneath your feet the rocks be rent,
Your swords and spears shall yet be shattered;
    Your kingdoms all be overthrown;

Your power and pride like dust be scattered,
    Like chaff before the whirlwind blown.

"Behold, I come"; ye nations, hearken:
    While yet his words rebuke and warn,
    Lest at His coming ye shall fear Him,
    Lest when ye see Him, ye shall mourn;
Seek ye His face while yet He's pleading,
    The Christ who on the cross has died,
    While yet His wounds are interceding
    To turn the wrath of God aside.

"Behold, I come"; the darkness lightens
    Above all sorrow and all fear;
Beyond the clouds the Daystar brightens,
    And our deliverance is near;
    The groaning earth awaits the hour
    When all the wrongs of time are past,
    And clothed with glory and with power,
    The King of kings shall reign at last.[5]

---

[5] Behold I come ... to give every man according as his work shall be. (Revelation 22:12)

AND HE SAITH, "FOLLOW ME"

"The cross awaits me"? Yes, I know.
"The night is dark"? But He is near.
"The path is rough"? His arm upholds.
"I cannot see"? But I can hear,
And where He leads I follow on;
He calls me, and I may not stay;
His strength is mine through all the days;
His light is sown along my way.
I know not where that way shall lead;
It matters not, so He shall guide,
Soonly, when the tempests come,
I feel His presence at my side.
When skies are bright above my head,
When smiling eyes with tears grow dim,
Through smiles or tears His peace is mine;
Tis joy enough to follow Him.
O loved Redeemer, loving Lord!
I hear Thy voice; it calleth me
Through joy and grief, through toil and pain,
To rest beyond the stormy sea;
O'er mount and valley, plain and stream,
Unto the place where I would be,
Unto the heaven where Thou hast gone,

I follow Thee – I follow Thee.[6]

---

[6] This spake he, signifying by what death he should glorify God. And when he had spoken this, he saith unto him, "Follow me". (John 21:19)

HITHERTO AND HENCEFORTH

Hitherto the Lord hath helped us,
Hitherto His hand hath led,
Hitherto His arm protected,
Hitherto His bounty fed;
Will His love desert us wholly,
Will His heart our need forget,
Will His presence clean forsake us,
Who hath never failed us yet?

Still His constant care surrounds us,
Keeping watch by day and night,
And His faithful promise tells us
We are precious in His sight.
He hath set no bounds, no limits,
To His ceaseless gifts of love;
He hath named no times, no seasons,
When His pledge untrue shall prove.

Let the Past we know assure us
Of the Present's certain aid,
Till the Future's dark forebodings
In the light of faith shall fade;
Still He hears ours supplications,
As our days our strength shall be;

And His grace is all-sufficient
For the needs of you and me.[7]

---

[7] Hitherto hath the Lord helped us. (1 Samuel 7:12)

YESTERDAY, TODAY AND FOREVER

But Yesterday men called the Father stern,
A righteous Judge, immutable, severe,
A jealous God, a terrible, a great
Whom guilty sinners held in trembling fear;
Who dwelt within the high and holy place
Where clouds and darkness wrapped His secret path,
About His head the judgment thunders rolled,
And blazed the lightnings of His awful wrath.
Today men say God is too kind to hate,
Too merciful to punish and too good,
Too loving to let any man be lost
And so deny His tender Fatherhood;
They have no sense of His great majesty
Nor any terror of His broken law,
They feel no fear of "All-Pervading Mind,"
No reverence and no adoring awe.
And when Tomorrow comes, what will they say?
What attributes assign Him and what name?
Lo! like a shadow they shall pass away,
But He endures, eternally the same.
They will not see that He has never changed
That man alone can turn and move and sway;
He was no sterner Yesterday than now,
He is no kinder now than Yesterday.

16

THE FIRST SONG SPARROW

"Oh, Spring is coming!" trills the robin bold
While still the wind is blowing bleak and cold,
And rags and tatters left by winter drear
in lingering fringes of the snow appear,
The cheery prophet of a good to be,
With no regard for what his eye may see
Hurls brave defiance at the stormy skies,
And sturdily repeats his prophecies.
But sudden comes a day of softer air
With still, warm sunshine lying everywhere;
The leafless trees a sharper shadow throw,
And vanished every vestige of the snow;
A silver haze blurs all the hard blue sky,
And veils the distant hills in mystery;
Then, gently, joyous, tender, and serene,
As if the promised good at last were seen,
I hear the first song-sparrow of the year
With confidence proclaiming, "Spring is here."

THE WORLD TO COME

There's a happier world than this
　Where all sorrow shall be o'er,
　Where no parting and no pain
E'er shall grieve our spirits more;
Where through all the blissful years
　Not a sigh shall vex our ears;
　God shall wipe away all tears
　In that happier world to come.

There's a brighter world than this
Where there shines nor sun nor moon,
　But the Lamb shall be the light
Through the cloudless, golden noon;
For there comes no darkness there,
　And across its glory fair
　Falls no shade of toil or care,
　In that brighter world to come.

There's a better world than this
　Where no evil enters in,
Hate or anger, pride or strife,
Thought of wrong, or deed of sin;
There no soul shall ever stray,
　For the curse is gone for aye;

Former things are passed away
In that better world to come.

There's a world more blest than this,
Where the King shall reign in peace.
Where with gladness we shall serve
And our songs shall never cease.
He is faithful; He is true;
Praise and glory are His due;
And He maketh all things new
In that blessed world to come.

Oh, that better world to come
Is our blessed heavenly home;
We shall walk in white with Jesus
In that brighter world to come.
And our hearts no more shall hunger,
And our feet no more shall roam,
In the land to which we journey,
That happier world to come.

WHO IS THIS THAT COMETH?

"Who is this that cometh," clothed in splendor and in light,
Victor over sin, and death, and all the hordes of night?
Lo! the meek Messiah who on Calvary was slain
Cometh now in judgment and in righteousness to reign.

"Who is this that cometh?" Son of man and Son of God,
Who for our salvation once the way of suff'ring trod,
Who for our deliverance once bore our pain and shame,
Blessing, praise and honor be forever to His name.

"Who is this that cometh?" Still His brow with thorns is scarred,
Wounded hands and wounded feet and face with sorrow marred;
Those who saw no beauty there once mocked Him with their scorn;
Now at His appearing all the tribes of earth shall mourn.

"Who is this that cometh?" King of Glory, King of kings;
Now to claim their heritage His ransomed hosts He brings,
Earth's remotest borders and the islands of the sea
Echo back the song they sing to Him who set them free.

Glory! Glory! Glory! for He cometh to His throne!
All the kingdoms of the earth He taketh for His own,
All the crowns of all the kings He weareth on His brow,
Every tongue shall hail Him Lord and every knee shall bow.

THE WAY TO ESCAPE

We beat with impatient hands
At the thorns of the wayside hedges
We bruise our feet on the stones,
And slip on the steep, rough ledges,
We stumble through quicksand and swamp
To impassable rivers flowing,
While alone we seek to find or make
Some safe, sure way for our going;
The way of our choice to a larger life
And into pleasanter places
With smoother paths for our feet to walk
In easier open spaces.

And we cry to the Lord to lead us out
From the struggle fierce and grim,
And out from the cloud that hides the sky
With its light grown murky and dim.
Not so can our soul escape
From the net of our strong temptations;
Not so can our hearts find rest
From our griefs and our tribulations;
But the Lord will make a way,
And we have only to follow;
He will lay the mountains low,

And level the swampy hollow;

He will bridge the deep, swift streams
And cleaves the rock before us;
He will hold up us with His hand,
And His shadowing wing spread o'er us.
Not always out will He make a road
When the strife grows fierce and grim,
But the way of escape may drive us in
To our refuge and rest in Him.
So welcome the bounds He hath set
To the way He hath planned for our going;
The hedge we may not break through,
And the deep, wide rivers flowing;

The sea that waits His word
To part its waves before us,
The darkness that hides our foes
'Neath the cloud that His hand spread o'er us;
Since they keep us the closer to Him,
Till, our will and our way forsaking,
We escape from the toils at last
By the way of the Lord's own making.
Not always out of our troublous times
And the struggles fierce and grim,
But in, deeper in, to our one sure rest,
The place of our peace, in Him.[8] [9]

---

[8] God will make a way to escape. (1 Corinthians 10:13)

[9] I am the way. (John 14:6)

IN FEBRUARY

Oh, they say it's growing colder every day,
That the winter's growing bolder every day
Since the bear's gone back to sleep
In his cavern dark and deep,
There'll be six weeks more of snowing,
Of freezing and of blowing—every day.
But the day's a little longer every day,
And the sun's a little stronger every day;
If we're patient for a while,
We shall see the summer smile,
And the buds will soon be showing,
For they're growing, growing, growing every day.
And the birds will soon be singing every day,
Northward now they'll soon be winging every day;
Though the frost is in the air,
There's a feeling everywhere
That the skies are growing clearer,
And the springtime's drawing nearer every day.

THOU REMAINEST

Thou remainest, Thou the changeless,
Though all else on earth may change,
Old joys fade, new griefs awaken,
Old things pass and new are strange,
Strength declines and footsteps falter
On the dark path we must face;
Thou remainest!Thou remainest!
God of glory and of grace.

Thou remainest,Thou our refuge,
When our hopes are all laid low;
Though our faith in man may weaken,
Faith in thee will stronger grow.
Heavy burdens weight our shoulders;
And the night brings no release;
Thou remainest! Thou remainest!
God of power and of peace.

Thou remainest, Everlasting,
When all else shall pass away;
Friends are gone and pleasures fail us,
And the clouds obscure our way,
Still Thy promise stands unshaken,
Life and death its trut shall prove;

Thou remainest! Thou remainest!
God of wisdom and of love.[10]

---

[10] Thou, O lord, remainest forever. (Lamentations 5:19)

SO SHALL HIS COMING BE

Whose are the whispers stealing
Out of the South and the North?
"Lo, from the secret chambers
The Christ is coming forth."
Whose are the voices crying
Out of the East and the West?
"Far in the desert hidden
Messiah takes His rest."

And one saith, "He is yonder,"
And one saith, "He is near."
And one at the door is calling,
"Behold Him! He is here."
Oh, go not out nor follow,
Ye seeking sons of men,
For not by observation
Will Jesus come again;

Not when your prophets plan it,
Not when your kings shall let;
Not as your time is reckoned,
Not on the day you set.
But as the lightning cometh,
Terrible, swift, and bright,

Cleaving the heavens asunder
And searing earth with its light.

Out of the storm'cloud leaping
Like a fiery swordblade's flash,
To the sound of the mighty waters
And the sevenfold thunders' crash,
A vision of flaming glory
That every eye shall see,
Lo, as the lightning cometh
So shall His coming be.[11]

---

[11] For as the lightning cometh ... so shall be the coming of the Son of Man. (Matthew 24:27)

SO LET IT BE

While peoples rise in anger
To set their brothers free,
While thrones and kingdoms totter.
And trembling tyrants flee;
'Mid death and desolation,
'Mid pestilence and pain.
'Mid famine, fire and earthquakes
That rend the hill and plain.
'Mid storms that shake the mountains
And winds that lash the sea–
O Lord, we cry in answer:
"Amen, so let it be."

We watch earth's fiercest tumult
With awe, but not with fear;
These are the signs that tell us
Thy day is drawing near.
Thou dwellest in the darkness,
Thou hidest in the cloud,
Thou ridest on the whirlwind,
Thou thunderest aloud;
Thou standest on the mountains,
Thou goest in the sea,
We hear Thy steps approaching–

Amen; so let it be.

Oh, haste Thy glad appearing,
The rising of Thy Sun,
When through Thy wide dominions
Thy will alone is done;
The long dispersed of Judah
And Israel's outcast band
Shall gather from all countries
Within their promised Land:
Then shall Thy whole creation,
From bondage know release,
Then shall the world's long warfare
End in a righteous peace;
Then shall Jehovah's glory
Cover the earth and sea,
And Christ be King forever.
Amen; so let it be.

THE SIGN OF THE SON OF MAN

I like to ponder that word of Scripture:
"Then shall the sign of the Son appear;"
To meditate on the many symbols
By which He speaks to His people here.

I like to wonder which sign is chosen
His glorious coming at last to bring;
Will it be the sword of our Victor Captain?
The shining crown of the conquering King?

Will it be the Star in the darkness gleaming
That led men's feet to His manager bed?
Or the rising Sun with its wings of healing
Breaking bright through the clouds of dread?

Will it be the Dove in the heavens flying
That heralds the Prince of Peace once more?
Or the smiting Stone that shall grind to powder,
And scatter the dust of the men of war?

Is it any of these? I muse and ponder
And closer, closer the page I scan;
These are the words the scribe has written;
It shall be "the sign of the Son of Man."

And what was the sign by His own rejected –
The sign of failure and death and loss?
The sign still spurned by a world that scorns Him?
The sign of the cross– the cross – the cross!

Is this the sign that shall show in heaven,
Rising in wrath where it rose in love?
Looming high in the skies of judgment,
A world of terror and doom above?

The sign of shame and the sign of glory,
Tenderest pity and love sublime,
Of a Lamb once slain, of a dying Saviour,
"Towering o'er the wrecks of time."

We do not know, but I muse and wonder;
He has not told us, we may but guess;
But I like to think that the cross is chosen,
The sign of His love and His righteousness.[12]

---

[12] And then shall appear the sign of the Son of man in heaven. (Matthew 24:30)

THE SIGN OF THE FIG TREE

Long had the tree been barren,
Lacking in leaf and fruit;
With branches withered and sapless,
Dried and dead from the root.
Weary and long was the winter
And earth was stormy and drear,
But now the tree grows tender,
And we know that summer is near.
For lo, in the withered branches
The sap begins to flow,
The boughs grow soft and supple,
And the first green leaf buds blow.
The tree of the Lord's own planting,
True Branch of David's Root,
Soon shall it bud and blossom
And fill the world with fruit.[13]

---

[13] And they saw the fig tree dried up from the roots. When her branch ... putteth forth leaves, ye know that summer is near. (Mark 11:20,13,28)

THE PERFECT MAN

The less we have in our scale, the more He puts in His;
Because His hand the balance holds, level and true it is.
His strength for all our weakness, His courage for our fear,
His love to fill the lonely heart, His voice for silence drear;
His light when darkness deeper grows, His hope for our despair,
His grace for loss and emptiness, for burden and for care:
His full supply for all our need, His comfort for our grief,
His patience for our puzzlements, His faith for unbelief;
His rest for toil and weariness, his joy for heavy hearts,
His wisdom for our ignorance, His balm for all our smarts;
His peace for every anxious thought, His armor for our strife.
The less we have, the more He gives, and so rounds out each life.
Because His hand the balance holds, level and true it is,
Till we shall stand complete in Him, with all the glory His.[14]

---

[14] Ye are complete in Him. (Colossians 2:10)

THE PASSING WORLD

Pass the sorrows of the world forever,
Fleeting trials and afflictions light;
As a troubled dream when one awaketh,
They shall be forgotten with the night.

Pass the pleasures of the world forever,
All delights the sons of men can know;
Lust of the flesh, the eyes that fail with longing
Music and laughter and the wine's red flow.

Pass the riches of the world forever,
Treasures of kings, the silver and the gold;
Lo, one shall heap them and another scatter,
No locks can keep, no clutching fingers hold.

Pass the labors of the world forever,
All the works the toil of men has wrought,
Urge of desire, the fret of futile striving,
Thrill of achievement – all shall come to nought.

Pass the beauties of the world forever,
Changeful sea and mighty mountain high,
Gleam of the moon across the rippling river,
All the fair loveliness of earth and sky.

Pass the glories of the world forever,
Pride of place and empty boast of power;
Books and their makers and their foolish wisdom,
Puppets of fame that strut their little hour.

Pass the empires of the world forever,
Crowns and conquering swords grow red with rust;
All their glittering pageantry's brief splendors,
All their tinsel trappings turn to dust.

Besides the changeless word of God forever,
Brighter growing as all else grows dim;
The world and all the lusts thereof are passing,
But they that do His will abide with Him.[15]

---

[15] For all that is in the world ... passeth away ... but he that doeth the will of God abideth forever. (1 John 2:16,17)

FROM FOREST TO FENDER

Log that burns to ashes gray
In my fireplace today,
Could you speak, what would you say
Of the years long passed away?
Had you tongue, would you be telling
Of your ancient greenwood dwelling;
Of your boughs' exultant swelling
When the swift sap, hurrying on,
Told of Winter's numbness gone?
How March winds, like trumpets blowing,
Stirred the larch plumes into growing,
Roused the chestnuts' snowy splendor
And the birch-tree tassels slender?
How the flowers, frail and tender,
Frightened at the stormy sound,
Stayed safe hidden under ground
Till, like fairy fingers strumming,
April's raindrops, lightly drumming,
Sounded the reveille gay
For the blossoms of the May:
"Snowdrop, — Crocus, — Violet, —
Are you wrapped in slumber yet?
Wake up, Daisy, Earth is waiting,
Bluebirds in the trees are mating:

Listen, Windflower, shy and sweet,
Breezes pass with flying feet,
Beckoning, calling, blithe and gay,
'Little comrade, come and play.'
Dandelion, please come up—
Meadow-sweet, and Buttercup,
Bright as newly-minted money;
Bees are calling for their honey;
You must hurry, Spring is here
And the ground looks bare and drear
Till you show your cheery faces,
Fill with light the gloomy places!"

THE ONLY WAY

Oh, the roads men make and the ways they take
To lead them up to heaven,
Since the first made man, with his easy plan,
From Eden's gate was driven!
Some turn and twist through fog and mist
With a plea of the Father's kindness;
Some only lead to a newer creed
For the cure of mortal blindness.

Some waver out in the sands of doubt
Where the trail is lost forever;
And some sink in to the swamps of sin
And cease their high endeavor.
Some stop before the open door
Of a Higher Critics' college;
And some stretch on in the twilight wan
Of Scientific Knowledge.

Some lose the way in the miry clay
Of the devil's specious treason;
Some wander lone in the vast unknown
Of philosophic reason.
But never a way will reach the goal,
Save the Way that God has given,

For "the blood-red road of the cross of Christ"

Is the only road to heaven.[16] [17]

---

[16] Jesus saith, ... I am the way, ... no man cometh unto the Father, but by me. (John 14:6)

[17] The blood red road of the cross of Christ. (Billy Sunday)

THE LORD'S RETURN

It is the glory of our lives
Above the glow of sun or star,
It is the lamp that lights our path,
The hope that beckons from afar.
It is the comfort for our griefs,
It is the joy that stays our tears,
It is the strength for all our toil,
It is the courage for our fears.

It is the promise of a morn
When earth's long, weary night is past,
It is the harbinger of peace
When earthly conflicts end at last.
It is the reign of righteousness,
It is the triumph of our faith,
It is the seal upon our love,
It is the vanquishment of death.

It is the guerdon of the years,
The goal of all the ages gone
That drew the prophets' wistful gaze
Beyond the darkness to the dawn.
Desire of all the Nations, come!
And bring the day for which we long;

Thou Sun of Righteousness, arise,
And heal all sorrow, right all wrong![18]

---

[18] To them that love his appearing. (2 Timothy 4:8)

LOOKING UNTO JESUS

Looking unto Jesus, we can follow on,
Treading in the pathway where His feet have gone;
So the darkness brightens, and the way grows plain;
So the burden lightens, and the weary pain;
With His smile to cheer us we need have no fear,
We can walk in safety though the foe be near.
Doubt is lost in trusting, toil forgot in rest;
Looking unto Jesus, we are ever blest.

Looking unto Jesus from the things of earth,
All its gifts and pleasures seem of little worth;
From our cares and trials let us turn away,
From the thorns that fret us through the long, hard day;
From these mortal changes to the land afar,
To the house eternal where our treasures are;
From our light afflictions to the things that last,
To the glory waiting when the gloom is past.

Looking unto Jesus all the way along,
So shall we be patient, so shall we be strong;
For the joy before us, counting all but dross,
With His power o'er us, we endure the cross.
Seeing Jesus nearer, growing more like Him,
Seeing heaven clearer as the world grows dim;

Strangers still and pilgrims, here awhile we bide;
Looking unto Jesus, we are satisfied.[19]

---

[19] Looking unto Jesus, the author and finisher of our faith. (Hebrews 12:2)

LO, HE COMETH!

Lo, He cometh! Lo, He cometh!
Not as once He came to earth–
Meek and gentle, poor and lowly,
Through the gates of human birth;
Not to walk with feet a wearied
Through a world of sin and pain,
By His own despised, rejected –
Lamb of God, for sinners slain.

Now in majesty He cometh,
Cloudy splendors wrap Him round;
Wake, ye dead, and list, ye living -
Hark! the trumpet's awful sound;
Now His face is like the lightning,
And His eyes are like a flame;
Lion of the Tribe of Judah,
Heaven and earth adore His name.

Lo, He cometh! Lo, He cometh!
Bride and Spirit echo "Come";
"Come to heal Thy hurt creation,
Come to take Thy people home;
Mount the throne, O Son of David,
Take the sceptre, Prince of Peace;

Come - and hush the drums' loud beating,
    Come - and bid all conflict cease.

Come - and furl the flags of warfare,
Come - and sheathe the nations' swords,
Come-and reign in truth and justice,
    King of kings, and Lord of lords.
    Come in power, come in glory,
Come to take Thy Kingdom - come!"
Even so, O King and Bridegroom,
    Even so, Lord Jesus, come!

A LITTLE WHILE

"A little while:" oh, ye who will not listen
Though He hath called you long,
To whom His message of reproof and warning
Is but an idle song,
A little while, and ye shall thirst and hunger
To hear His gracious word,
When ye shall call upon the rocks and mountains
To hide you from the Lord.

A little while - oh, comfort one another,
All ye who mourn, with this,
The promise of His presence and His likeness
In everlasting bliss;
A little while and He who rose triumphant
Shall call His dead to rise,
And we who live and those whom death has taken
Shall meet Him in the skies.

A little while, and He that cometh will come,
And will not tarry more;
Blessed are we if He shall find us watching
Beside the open door.
A little while, so little, oh, so little!
He bids us patient be

Until the clouds shall part, the shadows vanish,
And we His face shall see.[20]

---

[20] A little while and he that cometh will come and will not tarry. (Hebrews 10:37)

I COME AS A THIEF

"Behold, I come as a thief-"
Oh, hark to the word of His warning,
He cometh, the Star of the Morning
   That heralds the light of the Sun;
Far spent is the night of our sorrow,
New comfort, new hope, let us borrow.
   For soon, on the glorious morrow,
The Great Voice shall say: "It is done."

"Behold, I come as a thief-"
And ere the dull world shall awaken,
The treasure of earth shall be taken,
   The salt of the earth and its light;
The dungeons of Death shall be riven,
The Bride to the Bridegroom be given,
   His jewels be ravished to Heaven,
   In silent and shadowy night.

"Behold, I come as a thief-"
And blessed are they that are watching,
That so their quick ears may be hearing
   The sound of His step as they wait;
But woe unto them that are sleeping,
Who, careless, their garments are keeping,

The dawn on their slumbers is creeping-
They waken, but waken too late.

THE BUTTERFLY

He that kills a worm
Kills a butterfly.
In the ugly form
Of the crawling thing
Folded lies the wing
That shall cleave the sky;
In the creeping worm
Doomed his way to plod
With no thought nor care
Higher than the sod,
Rests the spirit form
Clothed in beauty rare,
That shall mount on high
Free of earth and air;
Once this shape outgrown
Comes the bliss of flight,
Glory and delight
To the clod unknown.
Spare the slow, dull form,
Pass the creature by,
He that kills a worm
Kills a butterfly.

Does the sluggish thing,

THE BUTTERFLY

Waiting dull and dumb,
Feel the folded wing,
Dream of joys to come?
Does he go his ways
Through the long, slow days,
Knowing that they tend
All to one sure end?

Worm, I thrill with thee!
Eager and elate,
Fettered here I wait
For the life to be.
Feel the folded wings
Faintly stir and rise,
While the clay that clings
Holds them from the skies.

Though the body wear
Old with fret and care
Though it weary grow
Of the treadmill round,
Plodding dull and slow,
Here upon the ground–
Grant, O Lord of Life,
That the wings of me,
May emerge from strife,
Sorrow, toil and pain,
With no spot nor stain;
May unmarred escape
From this mortal shape.
May I ever strive
These to keep alive,
These from death to save

And the body's grave;
Patient may I bide,
Though unsatisfied,
Still content to stay
My appointed day,
Till the shrouded soul,
Loosed from dark and dole,
From the clay that clings—
Chrysalis that holds,
Hampers and enfolds—
Spreads at last its wings,
Evermore to be
One with life and Thee.

THE HEAVENLY BRIDE

The Heavenly Bride is waiting for her Lord,
And long and slow the lonely years have been,
She cons the promise for her comfort given,
His "I will come", again and yet again;
Repeated to her loving, longing soul;
She wears His graces in her mind and heart,
She treasures all the precious gifts He sends,
Yet is she sad, for they are still apart.
But while she keeps His word of patience here
He waits with her for love's appointed hour,
Preparing home and throne and robe and crown,
That she may share His glory and His power.
And some day, while she pores upon His word,
And smiles through tears to think how His great love
Has dowered her with riches while she waits,
His voice will call her from the clouds above;
And she will spring to meet Him, and forget
How long He tarried in the Heavenly Place
In that deep rapture of fulfilled desire,
When she shall dwell with Him and see His face.[21]

---

[21] The voice of my beloved! behold he cometh ... Rise up, my love, my fair one, and come away ...
until the day break and the shadows flee. (Song of Songs 2:8,13,17)

GRACE ABOUNDING

Oh, the sorrows in the world today -
More than all the sorrows passed away;
Over all the mourning earth,
Grief hath banished song and mirth,
But His grace is deep enough to cover them.

Oh, the sinning in the world today,
As the wicked take their evil way;
Great iniquities abound,
All the groaning earth around,
But His grace is wide enough to cover them.

Oh, the terror in the world today,
As the shaken things of earth pass away;
Dread by day and fear by night
Spoil the sleep and dim in the light,
But His grace is high enough to cover them.

Oh, this mighty grace is ours today,
Though the earth and all therein pass away;
In the midst of woe and sin,
He will give us peace within,
For His grace is great enough to cover them.

His grace is deep enough to cover them;
His grace is wide enough to cover them;
No fear has ever been,
No sorrow and no sin,
For His grace is great enough to cover them.[22]

---

[22] Where sin abounded, grace did much more abound. (Romans 5:20)

THE EVERLASTING LOVE

Though we may waver,
He remaineth steadfast,
And all His words are sure;
From everlasting unto everlasting
His promises endure.
Though we may wander,
He will not forsake us,
Truer than earthly friend;
He never fails our trust,
For having loved us,
He loves unto the end.
Unto the end we
Doubt Him and deny Him,
We wound Him, we forget;
We set some earthly idol up between us
Without one faint regret.
And when it falls or
Crumbles, and in anguish
We seek this changeless Friend,
Lo! He receives us, comforts
And forgives us, and loves us to the end.[23]

DAILY WITH YOU

He is daily with us, loving, loving, loving;
Longing to befriend us, waiting but to bless;
Yet we bear our burdens, weary and discouraged,
And endure our sorrows, lonely, comfortless.

He is daily with us, pleading, pleading, pleading:
"Come, ye heavy-laden; come to me and rest,"
Yet we struggle onward, tempted, failing, sinning,
By the hosts of evil beaten and oppressed.

He is daily with us; calling, calling, calling,
Warning us to follow while we have the Light;
Yet we walk in darkness, sick with doubt and terror,
And bemoan our stumbling, and bewail the night.

He is daily with us, blessing, breaking, giving,
Asking but to feed us with the living Bread;
Yet we wander, seeking what earth cannot give us,
Hungering and thirsting, fainting and unfed.

Jesus, daily with us, though we grieve and slight Thee
Bear with us yet longer; leave us not, we pray.
Light of God, still leading, love of God, still pleading,

Christ, still interceding, stay with us today![24]

---

[24] I was daily with you. (Mark 14:49)

WHEN THE LEAVES FALL

When sunny days and frosty nights
Have wrought their mystic alchemies,
With amber warp and woof of flame
They weave their Orient tapestries;
And where the leafy tents of green
All summer long their shadows cast,
October's gay pavilions stand
Till levelled by November's blast.
Green leaves and golden—fair were they;
But beautiful, when they are gone,
The changing pageant of the skies,
The drifting clouds, the rose of dawn;
And, when those splendid curtains fall
That nightly foiled the peeping stars,
I note the blaze of sunset fires
And catch the ruby glow of Mars;
I see pale Venus' lamp of pearl
Across the purpling heavens' arch
Flash signal to the hosts of night
To recommence their stately march,
And watch while world on radiant world
With answering gleam wheels into place,
Until the fiery dot-and-dash,
Far-glimmering, fills the deeps of space,

So doth the near obscure the far,
The earthly hide the heavenly view,
And life must oft some glory lose
Ere we can see the stars shine through.

THE SONG OF RUNNING WATER

The song of running water; adown the mountain side
The brown brook hurries to its tryst like bridegroom to his bride,
It tinkles through the frosty night and babbles all the day,
And foams in wild impatience at each hindrance by the way,
Till at the wood's dusk entrance it checks its arrowy rush
To list the sighing of the pines, the vespers of the thrush;
It glides between its mussy banks in ripples sweet and cool,
Or pauses for the trout to leap in shadowy, rock-girt pool;
Then, "Follow—follow—follow!" it calls with laughing pure,
It sings the song of liberty, untrammeled, joyous, pure.

The song of running water: the meadow stream in tune
With all the sounds of summer and the golden lights of June;
It rests in clear, dark shallows beneath the dreaming trees,
Still mirror for the drifting fleets of heaven's argosies,
It purls in mimic eddies around the larger stones
And croons its lullaby of peace in lilting undertones;
"Oh, hush! Oh, hush!" it whispers to the trailing grasses green,
And shy forget-me-nots that o'er its lazy current lean.
Who would not loiter with it along its winding ways?
It sings the song of idleness and long, bright, happy days.

I have not learned its language, I do not know its speech,
And dead to me the secrets of the wonders it would teach.

Nor shall I ever comprehend till, past all pain and strife,
I wake where from the throne of God springs out the stream of life.
When all Eternity is ours and measured Time is o'er,
And finite in the Infinite is merged for evermore,
We shall not need its symbols and they shall cease to be;
We read as it is written: "There shall be no more sea"
No storm-tossed breakers, white with foam, no deadly undertow,
No ever-restless waves in that fair land to which we go;

No shifting sands, no ebbing tide, salt as our sorrow's tears,
No sunken rocks, no stranded ships, through all the deathless years.
But still the river runneth, to greet me with its song,
The music immemorial that I have loved so long.
With sound of many waters the crystal flood shall flow
And I shall find, in that clear voice, all voices that I know.
There shall the clue be given that eludes me here on earth:
These murmurs, half-articulate, of longing, grief and mirth,
The strange, wild, baffling harmonies from meadow, mount and wood,
Are blended there and reconciled, made plain and understood.

The song of running water: the river's chanted hymn
From canyon walls that soar aloft like vast cathedral dim;
And where its leaping cataracts fling high their rainbow spray,
Like some great organ's solemn tones its rolling thunders play.
The valleys robe themselves in beauty wheresoe'er it flows,
And in its path the wilderness shall blossom as the rose.
Beside it shall the hungry a dwelling place prepare,
And plant the vines and sow the fields and reap their fruitage fair,
Past cities filled with toilers and grimy factory slaves,
With rush of mighty waters, soft sweep of racing waves,

It turns the wheels of labor and bears the ships to sea,
And sings the song of industry, untiring, glad and free.

But brook, or stream, or river, whatever name it bears,
That song can soothe my restless moods and charm away my cares,
And oft when waking weariness would hold me far from sleep,
The memory of its melody has lulled to slumber deep.
Yet is its meaning all unknown, its thought a mystery
Though bird and wind and forest have each a word for me;
The fields are friendly comrades, the sky a beckoning hand,
But oh! the murmuring water I cannot understand.

I hush my heart to listen, I hear its haunting strain,
A voice from that lost Paradise we may not here regain.
The scattered notes, the semi-tones, the broken chords, half-heard,
The plaintive minor cadences by jarring discords blurred,
Shall prove but parts of one great whole, a wondrous symphony
That our dull ears can never hear this side Eternity;
But there attuned to Heaven's tones, our finer sense shall feel
What Eden's muted echoes are striving to reveal,
Complex and many-sided, with mingled meanings rife,
The Song of Running Water is but the Song of Life.

MY TREES

They do not stand in forest glade
With moss and fern about their feet,
Instead, they cast their pleasant shade
As warders of a village street;
Not theirs the brooding silence deep
From dawn to dusk, from dark to day,—
They hear the housewife's cheery calls,
The shouts of children at their play.

But sun and rain are kind to them,
Their leaves dance with the dancing breeze,
And through the changes of the years
I watch and love my neighbor trees.
I thrill with them when spring returns
To rouse them from their peaceful dreams
With some elusive message borne
By softer airs or murmuring streams;

When through the slowly lengthening days,
All heedless of the lingering cold,
The first impatient birds arrive
With wind-blown feathers, blithe and bold;
They sing amid the reddening boughs
And choose the sites for future homes,

Serenely sure, through snow or sleet
Or pelting rain, that summer comes.

I joy with them in long, bright days
When leafy depths with life o'erflow;
The squirrels race from tree to tree
And chatter madly as they go;
Through sultry noons and stifling nights,
From their cool shade the locust shrills
His oft repeated prophecies
Of heat that blights and drought that kills;

On one long branch above my roof
The hang-bird's cradle sways and swings,
And when the hungry fledglings wake,
With raucous calls the morning rings:
Then, fluttering down from stair to stair,
With many a slip and anxious cry,
All spotted breasts and stumpy tails,
The baby robins learn to fly.

I rest with them when autumn frosts
Have changed their sober green array
To gorgeous garments, bright as brief,
That fade and fall from day to day,
Revealing, through a thinning veil,
Mute memories of summer past,
The small forsaken homes of song,
Frail playthings for the winter's blast;

And when the early darkness comes,
The moonbeams weave, with elfin grace,
Across the looms of leafless twigs

Their magic mesh of shadow-lace.
I hope with them 'neath wintry skies,
Nor do I feel them sad or chill;
Austere but beautiful they stand
And read to me a lesson still;

They patient bide the waiting-time
Of glory gone and beauty lost,
Assured that not a leaf shall fall
And not a bough by storm be tossed,
Save but as part of God's great plan
For them and me and all the earth,
And that a richer, fuller life
Shall follow on this seeming dearth.

One tells me of the mountain slopes,
And one of ocean's myriad moods,
And one of some fair mirror-lake
Enshrined in woodland solitudes;
My feet may never wander far
To seek such varied joys as these,
But pent, like them, in village street,
I am content—I have my trees.

THE FLIGHT OF THE AIRSHIP

Ahoy! Yacht Butterfly, loosing your moorings,
Whither, whither, away?
Clearing the tops of the wind-tossed clover,
Where do you cruise today?

'Ware the web of the yellow spider
Lurking beside the stream!
There by the cat-tails something's moving,
Flickering flash and gleam;

Quick! up sail and away, O Captain!
This is a craft to fear,—
Armored cruiser and merciless pirate,
Dragonfly buccaneer!

Signal in passing the heavily-laden,
Lumbering freighter-bees,
Riding at anchor or taking cargo,
Moored in the apple-trees;

Steer you now for the upper currents,
Northerly with them swing:
Here go the clipper-built ships of the Air-Line,
Birds of the tireless wing.

Far beneath you, in shine and shimmer
Map of the world's unrolled;
Burnished buttercups glow and glisten,
Field of the Cloth of Gold;

Riotous breezes are blowing the blossoms,
Wheat-heads ripple and bow,
Foam-like the green of the poplars whitens
Under your dancing prow.

Oh! the day is a dream of beauty,
Long are the hours and bright,
Slowly, slowly its radiance softens,
Dims and darkens to night;

Swallows, tracing their curves of beauty,
Circle the sapphire dome;
Turn you, turn you, O Butterfly Skipper!
Tack for the Port of Home.

Hoarse and plaintive the whippoorwill's crying
Rings from the wooded crest,
Hark to the call of the bo'sun Robin,
Piping the world to rest;

Faintly fragrant the primrose opens,
Fire-flies winking nigh;
Droning beetles plow clumsily homeward,
Humming-bird-moth scuds by.

Cool and dewy the shadows lengthen,
Stretching across the vale,
A silver shallop, the new moon's floating

Out where the West grows pale.

Where shall the fitful zephyrs bear you?
Where does your harbor lie?
There where the masts of the pine-trees tower,
Looming against the sky?

Nearer, nearer the slack tide drifts you,
Voyage is almost past;
Furl your sails, O Butterfly Captain!
Haven is reached at last.

EMMANUEL

"God with us" in this world of sin,
This life of weakness and of woe:
His love, His power and His strength
With us, wherever we may go,
Since Jesus came to earth to dwell
And be for aye Emmanuel.

No weary days, no starless nights,
No sorrow deep, no trial sore,
But we can feel His presence near,
"God with us", now and evermore;
Since He hath come to earth to dwell
Whose name is still Emmanuel.[25]

---

[25] They shall call His name Emmanuel, 'God with us.' (Matthew 1:23)

"WHAT ARE THESE WOUNDS?"

What are these marks on Thy brow, Lord Jesus, —
Brow that were else so fair?
Crown of a King or the High Priest's mitre
Could not have left them there!"
"Laid on my head, all the guilt of thy sinning
Pierced it, bowed it with shame,
That my redeemed ones might lift up their fore-heads
Sealed with my Father's name;
That I might crown them who follow me ever,
Treading the path I trod,
Leading them up out of great tribulation
Into the kingdom of God."

"What are these wounds in Thy hands, Lord Jesus, —
Hands that were else so fair?"
"Knowest thou not that the Lord who bought thee
Ever that sign must bear?
So must thy name on my palms be graven
Making thee mine for aye;
Only the hands that were pierced could lift thee
Out of the miry clay,
Lift thee, and carry, and hold, and lead thee
Into the Promised Land;
Safe I keep, and no man shall pluck thee

71

Out of my wounded hand."

"What are these prints on Thy feet, Lord Jesus, —
Feet that were else so fair?"
"I walked the path that my sheep must follow, —
Many a thorn was there;
Thieves and robbers had torn and smitten,
Hirelings failed to keep,
I am the Shepherd who came but to save them,
Giving my life for the sheep.
Still I am seeking until I shall find them
Whithersoever they stray;
Only the feet that were pierced can guide them
Into the peaceful way."

"What is the scar on Thy side, Lord Jesus, —
What could have left it there?"
"My heart must break 'neath the weight of earth's sorrow
Ere I thy griefs could share;
I must drink deep of the world's cup of anguish,
Draining its wormwood and gall,
From Eden's curse to the kiss of betrayal, —
Bitterest drop of it all.
Hearts that I died for yet doubt and deny me,
Grieving their truest Friend;
Only a heart that was pierced and broken
Ever could love to the end.[26]

---

[26] And one shall say unto him, What are these wounds in thine hands? Then he shall answer, Those with which I was wounded in the house of my friends. (Zechariah 13:6)

THE VISION

There is a vision that the proud world needs: —
The world that says, "I see", and yet is blind;
That says, "I know", and yet is ignorant,
And in its progress leaves the Christ behind;
The world that boasts its wealth, and yet is poor;
That says, "I have", yet is not satisfied;
The world that says, "I will", and yet is weak;
And in its wisdom sets the Christ aside.

This is the vision that the sad world needs:
The vision of the Christ upon the cross,
The Christ whose tender hand its woes can heal,
Whose pitying heart can comfort every loss;
Ten thousand times ten thousand broken hearts!
Yet His has borne the agony of all,
And now He waits with outstretched hands of love
Till they shall hear and answer to His call.

This is the vision that the dark world needs:
The vision of the Christ who died for men,
And from whose cross there radiates a light
Whose brightness never shall be quenched again,
Oh, fearful night of anguish and of sin!
Oh, dreadful darkness where no ears arise!

His truth alone can guide the groping soul,
His touch alone unseal the blinded eyes.

This is the vision that the mad world needs:
The vision of the Christ uplifted high
Above its battlefields of blood and death,
Where those stark shapes in foul corruption lie,
Ten thousand times ten thousand ghastly slain,
An open sore that bleeds and will not cease;
Yet this Man's wounds avail to staunch that wound,
If but the world would take His offered peace.

This is the vision; but the world sweeps on,
With speed and clamor filling eye and ear;
There is no vision for the wilful blind,
There is no voice for those who will not hear.
The world is wretched, naked, poor and blind,
Yet knows it not, and chants its helpless creeds;
Unseen, unheard, still waits the patient Christ,
This is the vision that the whole world needs.[27]

---

[27] Where there is no vision, the people perish. (Proverbs 29:18)

THE UNKNOWN NAME

We shall be ever seeing
New beauties in our Lord,
New majesty, new sweetness
In God's eternal Word;

New mysteries unfolding
When old have been revealed,
Old wonders comprehended
To show still more concealed.

We shalt be ever finding
New marvels in The Christ,
For which our deepest knowledge
Has never yet sufficed;

Exhaustless graces flowing,
More loveliness and more,
And always through the ages
New greatness to adore;

New riches, new compassions
And fresh reserves of love;
Infinities of wisdom
Our highest thought above.

All His dear Names unnumbered
We shall exalt, adore;
Yet, for our fullest homage
There will be one Name more.

For, though we learn forever,
One thing may not be known,
One glory, all transcendent,
Shall still be His alone.

Depth beneath all depths fathomed,
Height above all heights scaled,
Word beyond all words uttered,
Paramount grandeur veiled:

Fragrance of hidden sweetness,
Glow of an unseen flame,
Grace of a secret beauty, —
Glorious Unknown Name![28]

---

[28] And he had a name written, that no man knew, but he himself. (Revelation 19:12)

THE STRANGERS

As unto the blind the colors
Of earth and sky and seas,
As unto the deaf the music
Of melodious harmonies,
As unto the dumb the sweetness
Of the songs they have never sung,
As unto the alien the welcome
In the words of another tongue,
So unto those who are strangers
To the covenants of grace,
Who are deaf to the voice of Jesus
And blind to the light of His face,
Who are dumb in the language of heaven
And have never been born again, —
To them the things of the Spirit
Are quite beyond their ken.
Oh, the peace and the joy they are missing!
Eternal and infinite loss,
If they seek not the life everlasting
And find not the way of the cross.[29]

---

[29] The natural man receiveth not the things of the Spirit God ... neither can he know them because they are spiritually discerned. (1 Corinthians 2:14)

THE SILENCE OF GOD

Jehovah saith no more; the voice of God hath ceased.
No more by vision or by dream, by prophet or by priest,
By ephod or by teraphim, by angel or by star,
By altar or by sacrifice, He speaketh from afar.

No more—He saith no more; the silent heavens wait;
The silent angels keep their watch beside the open gate;
The silent Christ bends low with tender, pitying face,
To see if one more soul on earth will seek God's offered grace.

Jehovah saith no more. Why should He speak again,
When His last word is echoing yet within the ears of men?
But they refuse to hear, and through the flying days
They eat and drink and buy and sell, and go their careless ways.

Jehovah saith no more. His last great Word is said
Till from the earth and sea His voice shall call the dead;
Till like the thunder's peal His judgment word is hurled
To shake with awful wrath the unbelieving world.

But now His voice is still. O ye whose hearts have heard,
Ye are the voice of God to speak His gracious word.
Repeat it to the sons of men, though they the call ignore,

For, save as ye shall speak His word, Jehovah saith no more.[30]

---

[30] God, who at sundry times and in divers manners spake in time past ... hath in these last days spoken ... by His Son. (Hebrews 1:1,2)

THE SHADOW OF THE CROSS

O Christ! Who once has seen Thy visioned beauty ~
He counts all gain but loss,
All other things are naught if he may win Thee
And share with Thee Thy cross.

And be on whom its shadow one hath fallen
Walks softly and apart;
He holds the master-key of joy and sorrow
That opens every heart.

The burdened souls that pass him on the highway
Turn back to take his hand,
And murmur low, with tear-wet eyes of anguish.
"You know—you understand."

And yet his heart no other can interpret.
His life is hidden, lone:
A holy seal is set upon his forehead,
And he is not his own.

O Cross of Christ! on me thy shade is resting,
Thy sacred marks I bear:
Earth holds for me no more of grief or gladness,
No anxious thought nor care;

Only henceforth, the bliss and pain commingled
Of sharing woes divine,
Of knowing I am called to eat His portion,
To drink His bitter wine.

Keep me forever, Lord, beneath that shadow,
Lest, haply, I should lose
My life for something less than Thy sweet service,
Or one dear pang refuse.

I WILL NOT BE AFRAID

I will trust Him, yea, I will trust
For He never hath failed me yet;
And never a day nor an hour,
But mine uttermost need is met,
Though I dwell in the midst of foes,
Yet there is my table spread,
And His presence wraps me round
And His wings are over my head.

Father and Infinite God,
My Refuge and Fortress Rock,
Where I hide from the tempest's wrath,
And feel not the earthquake shock.
So I bide with a soul serene
And a heart that is undismayed
He is my Strength and my Shield;
Of whom shall I be afraid?

I will not be afraid, for I know
That He keepeth me safe from harm,
And He shall defend His own
With a strong and a stretched-out arm.
Though I grope in perilous paths,
In darkness and danger and doubt,

I know, as He brought me in,
So He surely will bring me out.

For the God I serve today
Is one with God of old;
Still doth He guide my steps
And still doth His hand uphold,
He giveth me rest from fear,
For one Him my mind is stayed,
He is the Strength of my life;
Of what shall I be afraid?

I will trust and not be afraid,
I have seen, I have heard, I have known,
This mighty and terrible God
Hath called me and made me His own.
"Dread not! Faint not!" He hath said,
"For the battle belongs to me,
Go forth with a song of praise,
And My victory thou shalt see."

And where I go He will go,
And He knoweth the way I take;
He is with me unto the end,
And He will not fail nor forsake,
They that trust in the Lord
Shall never be moved nor swayed,
"Fear not!" He hath said unto me,
And why should I be afraid?[31] [32]

---

[31] What time I am afraid, I will trust in Thee. (Psalm 56:3)

[32] I will trust and not be afraid. (Isaiah 12:2)

THE RIVER'S LULLABY

When the evening shadows chase away the light,
And the golden sunbeams fade before the night,
Flows a quiet river, broad and calm and free;
Hear it softly singing, "Come! oh, come with me,
To the Sleepy Harbor, far and far away,
Where, when day is over, all the children stay;
There a lovely country waits thy loitering feet—
'Tis the Baby's Dreamland, fair and bright and sweet!"
Sway the tangled rushes, float the silver lilies,
Bend the trailing willows o'er the rippling stream.
Listen, baby, listen to the river's singing—
Let its music mingle with thy peaceful dream.
Gently will the river bear thee on its breast;
Stars will light my darling to the land of rest,
Short and safe the journey,—sleep, and that is all:
"Hasten, baby, hasten," hear the river call;
"Fairies wait thy coming, lovely tales to tell,
And the flower bells' chiming on the wind will swell:
Green are all the meadows for thy tiny feet,
And above thee watches an angel fair and sweet."
Sway the tangled rushes, float the silver lilies.
Bend the trailing willows o'er the rippling stream:
Listen, baby, listen to the river's singing,
Let its music mingle with thy peaceful dream.

IN THE WINTER WOODS

In the desolate forest the snow-wreaths cover
The dead things over with ermine pall,
And the bare brown cup of a nest forsaken,
Where no birds waken with jocund call,
Is filled with the silence of cold flakes drifting
And lightly sifting, that o'er it fall.

But neither of grief nor of gloom 'tis telling,
This empty dwelling where song is stilled;
It whispers yet of a day of gladness
Untouched by sadness, with joyance thrilled,
Of a dream come true, of a finished story,
The rainbow glory of Hope fulfilled.

'Twas a cup poured full of the wine of pleasure,
Unstinted measure o'erflowed its brim,
And the near, and the far, and the new, the olden.
The gray, the golden, to Earth's wide rim,
Had each a share in that joy of living,
A beauty giving no cloud might dim.

For your hearts were in tune with the great Earth Mother's,
O Little Brothers of Airy Flight!
No fear of the future your thoughts invading,

Of green leaves fading or skies less bright;
Since you knew, ere the chill of the frost could scare you,
Your wings would bear you beyond its blight.

O wee, brave souls of a cheer unfailing!
How unavailing the loads we bear;
And oft I long, when I hear you singing,
Your far flight winging through sunlit air,
To rise, like you, to the Heavenly places,
In wide, free spaces to lose my care.

But our thoughts may mount as you rise, and follow
Like homing swallow that seeks her mate,
As you lead them up through the low clouds trailing,
Its glory veiling, to Heaven's gate,
From the Land of the Perfect Peace to borrow
The balm of sorrow, for which we wait.

Dear earth-born dwellers, akin to Heaven,
To you is given a mission sweet;
Between them ever a chain you're weaving,
The blue depths cleaving on pinions fleet,
And the notes you glean at that radiant portal,
From songs immortal, your own repeat.

In the hush of the woods, by their memories haunted
A land enchanted, where dreams have birth,
I linger long, for I fain would capture
The wraith of rapture, the ghost of mirth;
Yet I know they are shut in their snowy prison,
Till Life, new-risen, shall wake the earth.

THE NAME OF JESUS

There is a name all names above,
Exalted names of Jesus,
It tells us of a Father's love,
The saving name of Jesus,
Is is the sinner's only plea,
The seal of his salvation;
It is the Christian's joyful hope,
His faith's secure foundation.

There is a name wherein we hide,
The fortress-name of Jesus,
The refuge where our souls may bide,
The mighty name of Jesus,
It was our father's dwelling place
And still for us availing;
Unshaken should its ramparts stand
Against the world's assailing.

There is a name by which we live,
The one great name of Jesus,
The daily triumph it will give,
The victor-name of Jesus;
It is the sword that smites our foes
With lightning stroke of splendor,

For every danger, every fear,
Our shield and our defender.

There is a name that lights our way,
The shining name of Jesus,
A star by night, a sun by day,
The wondrous name of Jesus;
It is a lamp that never dims
Through mists of time far gleaming,
The only light steps to guide
Thro' death's dark portal streaming.

There is a name that fills our ears,
The lovely name of Jesus,
That stills our sighs and stays our tears,
The blessed name of Jesus;
It is a precious ointment poured,
All earthly sorrows healing,
The name in which alone we trust,
The grace of God revealing.

There is a name—men scorn it now—
The lowly name of Jesus,
But at that name they yet shall bow,
The kingly name of Jesus;
It is the song of hosts redeemed,
Its fadeless story telling;
With them may we forever praise
The Name all names excelling.[33] [34]

---

[33] Thou shalt call his name Jesus, for he shall save his people from their sins. (Matthew 1:21)

[34] A name which is above every name. (Philippians 2:9)

NO MORE

These the saddest words of earth: "No more, no more,"
With a hopeless desolation their echoes running o'er,
Every coming morrow brings new and newer sorrow,
Loss on losses crowding till the world with woe is filled;
Not all our crying, nor all our anguished sighing
Can give us back the lighter of voices that are skilled;
For our vain imploring there is no restoring,
There is no rebuilding of the ruined past;
Still for all our yearning the dead are unreturning,
No lost treasures at our feet by Time's swift tide are cast,
"No more—no more," the bells of doom are tolling,
Their dull reverberations through the stricken world are rolling.
"None shall see again the glory of earth's vanished yesterday;
No more—never any more—for the former things have passed away,"
These the gladdest words of heaven: "No more, no more,"
With unspeakable rejoicing their accents running o'er,
No more crying nor any anguished sighing,
No more lonely weeping to fill the weary night,
No more bitter sorrow on any coming morrow,
No more hopeless yearning for loved ones more turning,
No more haunting memories that sear the heart in vain;
No more sad imploring for some lost joy's restoring,
No more death forever, no hunger, and no pain;
"No more—no more," the raptured voices calling,

The music of their echoes on the stricken world is falling,
None shall know again the terrors of earth's vanished yesterday;
No more—never any more—for the awful curse of sin has passed away.

THE PRAYER IN THE NIGHT

Sometimes I wake with dark and quiet around me,
And swift across my vision, like a light,
Flashes the face of one I know who suffers,
Or one whom sorrow newly touched last night,
Perhaps, for just that moment and that purpose,
There lacks a link in God's great chain of prayer;
So, lest the chain be weakened by my silence,
Or break because I fail to do my share,
I shape the link, and know the Spirit's fire
Will forge it into place and weld it there.

THE PRAYER OF MARTHA

Lord, I am cumbered with so many cares,
I needs must serve throughout the livelong day,
Must keep the little clinging hands from harm,
And guide the stumbling feet along the way,
Till weary head and heart may take their rest
When prattling voices hush at set of sun.
O Jesus, Master! At Thy feet, for me,
Keep Mary's place till Martha's work is done.

THE RICHES OF HIS GRACE

Oh, like the air about us that we breathe,
As limitless and all-encompassing;
And like the earth beneath us that we tread,
As strong, as solid, and unvarying;
And like the sky above, where sun and stars
In old, unalterable orbits wing;
So is Thy grace to us, O God of grace!
Pledge of Thy mercy, promise of Thy might
Changeless through all the sorrows of the day,
Changeless through all the terrors of the night,
A present peace, a certain comforting,
Sustaining joy and everlasting light.[35]

---

[35] The exceeding riches of His grace. (Ephesians 2:7)

ROSES AND SNOWFLAKES

Love of the Lord in the roses
Crimson and white,
Wonder of color and perfume,
Joy and delight.

Love of the Lord in the snowflakes
When snowflakes must fall,
Over the bier of the roses
Laying a pall.

Love—in the light or the darkness,
Harvest or seed,
Leaf that is greening or fading
Flower or weed.

All is of love; shall we doubt it
Though roses are dead,
When He gives us the marvelous beauty
Of snowflakes instead?[36] [37]

---

[36] There is as much of God's love in a snowflake as in a roseleaf. (Lucy Larcam)

[37] Shall we receive good at the hand of the Lord and ... not evil? (Job 2:10)

THE SHINING OF THE STARS

When the evils of earth were greatest
The Christ-child came from afar;
When the night of the world was darkest
Shone forth the Bethlehem Star;
Glory and peace was its message,
Love and goodwill to men—
A peace beyond their making,
A love beyond their ken.

Long has the vexed world waited
The peace that He came to bring;
Long have the turbulent peoples
Looked for a righteous king;
Long has His sad creation
Waited redemption's word;
Long have His faithful servants
Watched for their absent Lord;

Long—but the time draws nearer,
The Bridegroom comes from afar;
When the night of the age is darkest
We shall see the Morning Star,
Evil is growing stronger,
And hearts are sick with fear;

But our hope is growing brighter,
For we know that the hour is near,

Faint in the dark skies gleaming,
Faint on the roaring seas,
But it heralds the dawn of glory
And it hastens the day of peace—
The glory, the peace He is bringing,
The King Who comes from afar;
And to him who overcometh
He will give the Morning Star.

SINCE YESTERDAY

Where has he gone since yesterday—
The friend who left us here?
Tonight he seems so far away
Who yester-eve was near.
No map of ours, on sea or land,
His journeyings may trace;
We only know he's reached his home
And seen his Father's face.

And oh! He knows since yesterday,
And he'll be learning fast;
The mists have all been cleared away;
The mysteries are past.
The sun of truth he sought so long
Unshadowed glows for him,
And nevermore one low'ring cloud
Its radiance may dim.

And he has grown since yesterday,
And he'll be growing still;
The bonds of time and sense and space
That irked his eager will,
Were dropped like shackles from the soul
In that first upward flight;

The weary body frets no more,
The spirit, freed and light.

O dear, familiar yesterday!
O sad and strange today!
Yet who would call the glad soul back
To rouse the resting clay?
Or who could wish that he might know
Our morrow's pain and strife,
When he who, once, so longed to live
At last has entered Life?

THAT DAY

That morn shall break as others break;
 The stars shall pale, the shadows flee;
Across the misty mountain-tops
The sun shall gild the sleeping sea;
The busy world shall wake once more
With smiles or sighs to greet the day,
 To eat and drink, to buy and sell,
 To scheme and toil, to sin and pray.

That morn shall break as others break;
 But ere the day its course has run
Full many a watching, waiting soul
Shall know the waiting-time is done.
 They see a sign no others see,
 And hail the long-expected day;
They hear a voice no others hear—
 "Haste, my beloved, come away."

That morn shall break as others break;
 But, ere another day shall dawn,
Where two were grinding, one is left;
Where two were sleeping, one is gone,
 "Behold, He comes," The Spirit saith;
O Earth, Earth, Earth! The message hear,

O blind and deaf! The sign discern;
Redeem the hours, the time is near.

TO BRING BACK THE KING

"Behold, I come quickly." Oh, hasten Thy coming,
    And fly on the tempest and ride on the cloud;
        Around us the rage of the storm increasing,
            The menacing roar of billow is loud;
        The earth holds refuge, the world has no helper,
And men's hearts are anxious and failing with fear;
    Repeat the assurance that fills us with comfort
When death and despair and destruction are near.

"Behold, I come quickly." So come, we beseech Thee;
        But what are we doing to hasten the day
    When earth shall be filled with the light of Thy glory,
            To bring back the King from the land far away?
        Are we sowing the seed on the field and way-side?
        Or reaping the harvests long waiting and white?
Are we keeping our lamps filled and shining and burning,
        And holding them high in the darkness of night?

"Behold, I come quickly." So come, we entreat Thee;
        But how we are helping to answer our prayer?
Do we gather the stumbling-blocks out of the high-way,
    And make smooth the path for the feet that walk there?
        Are we doing Thy will? Are we giving Thy message
    To souls Thou hast loved and redeemed on the cross?

Do we show forth Thy grace to the sad world around us?
The patience in trial, Thy comfort in loss?

We watch for the signs and we love Thine appearing,
We long for the peace that kingdom will bring,
But what are we doing to hasten Thy coming?
And how are we helping to bring back the King?[38] [39]

---

[38] Behold, I come quickly ... Even so, come, Lord Jesus. (Revelation 22:7,20)

[39] Why are ye the last to bring the king back? So they sent this word ... Return thou ... So the king returned." (Samuel 19:12,15)

THE UNFINISHED SONG

When the heavenly hosts shall gather and the heavenly courts shall ring
With the rapture of the ransomed, and the New Song they shall sing,
Though they come from every nation, every kindred, every race,
None can ever learn the music till he knows God's pardoning grace,
All those vast eternities to come will never be too long
To tell the endless story and to sing the endless song;
"Unto Him who loved us and who loosed us from our sin"—
We shall finish it in heaven, but 'tis here the words begin,
"Unto Him who loved us"—we shall sing it o'er and o'er,
"Unto Him who loved us"—we shall love it more and more;
"Unto Him who loved us"—song of songs most sweet and dear;
But, if we would know it yonder, we must learn the music here.

Here, where there was none to save us, none to help us, none to care,
Here, where Jesus came to seek us, lost in darkness and despair,
Here, where on that cross of anguish He redeemed us from our sins,
Here, where first we knew the Saviour, it is here the song begins,
Here, amid the toils and trials of this fleeting earthly life,
Here, amid the din and turmoil of this troubled earthly strife,
Here, in suffering and sorrow, here in weariness and wrong;
We shall finish it in heaven, but 'tis here we start the song,
"Unto Him who loves us"—we must sing it every day,
"Unto Him who loves us"—who is Light and Guide and Way;
"Unto Him who loves us"—and who holds us very dear;

If we'd know it over yonder, we must learn the music here.

There will be no silent voices in that ever-blessed throng;
There will be no faltering accents in that hallelujah song;
Like the sound of many waters shall the mighty paean be
When the Lord's redeemed shall praise Him for the grace that set them free,
But 'tis here the theme is written; it is here we tune our tongue;
It is here the first glad notes of joy with stammering lips are sung,
It is here the first faint echoes of that chorus reach our ear;
We shall finish it in heaven, but our hearts begin it here,
"Unto Him who loved us"—to the Lamb for sinners slain,
"Unto Him who loved us"—evermore the joyful strain;
"Unto Him who loved us"—full and strong and sweet and clear;
But, if we would know it yonder, we must learn to sing it here.[40] [41]

---

[40] Unto Him that loved us, and washed us from our sins in His own blood ... be glory and dominion forever and ever. (Revelation 1:5,6)

[41] And no man could learn that song but the ... redeemed from the earth." (Revelation 14:3)

THE WATCHERS

Long past is the evening; the watchers
Looked forth from their windows in vain,
They saw but the darkening shadows
As night settled down o'er the plain.
The midnight is gone, with its blackness
Unlightened by sun or by star;
Though the cry sounded forth, "He is coming,"
The Bridegroom still tarried afar.
The cock-crowing ceased and the silence
Fell deep and profound as before;
The watchers, aroused by the summons,
Sank back into slumber once more.
Now the long night is done, and the watchers
Look forth with a gladness new-born;
Though He came not at even or midnight,
His promise holds good for the morn,
The East is still shrouded with shadows,
The storm-clouds are gathering fast;
But lo! Where they part for a moment,
The Star of the Morning at last![42]

---

[42] Watch ye therefore; for ye know not when the Master of the house cometh, at even, or at midnight or at the cock-crowing, or the morning. (Mark 13:35)

WHAT I TELL YOU IN DARKNESS

What I tell you in darkness, that speak ye in light.
My words of consolation, my songs in the night;
When the shadows have vanished and the morn breaks again,
Go tell what I have told you to the children of men.

What I tell you in darkness, when the wind whips the sea,
When the waves overwhelm you and you cry unto me;
When my voice stills the tempest, my words calm your fear,
That tell to your brother, their fainting hearts cheer.

What I tell you in darkness, when I answer your call
When you walk in rough places, and stumble and fall;
When my word lights your pathway, a lamp to your feet,
To those who fall beside you, my message repeat.

What I tell you in darkness, hold fast in your heart,
From the desert-place of waiting, where I call you apart,
From the stillness and the shadow where you were so blest
Go forth and speak to others who know not my rest.

What I tell you in darkness, in the long night of fear,
When I wake and watch beside you, and no other is near;
In the gloom of the Garden, where you echo my prayer—
That speak to those around you who agonize there.

WHEN JESUS STOOD STILL

The Son of man must go as it was written:
Be mocked and scourged, in agony must die;
Steadfast He set His face toward shame and spitting,
Yet could He halt at Bartimaeus' cry.
This too was written; from the world's foundation
It was ordained that here the two should meet,
That at the wayside beggar's prayer for mercy
The Son of God just here should stay His feet.

No powers of earth or hell can change His purpose,
Or turn aside the thing He hath decreed;
All things concerning Him must be accomplished,
So must He hear the sinner's city of need;
So must He hearken unto thee who trusts Him,
This too concerns Him, for He loveth thee;
Come thou in faith, the world of doubt defying,
And all that doubting world must wait thy plea.[43] [44]

---

[43] All things that are written ... concerning the Son of Man shall be accomplished. (Luke 18:31)

[44] And Jesus stood still. (Mark 10:49)

WHERE IS THE PROMISE?

Where is the promise of His coming?
It is settled in the counsel of the Lord;
By prophet, saints and sages
Through the slow march of the ages
It was blazoned on the pages of His Word

.

Where is the promise of His coming?
It was given unto Israel of old,
And through sore humiliation
It is still their consolation
While they wait the restoration long foretold.

Where is the promise of His coming?
It is hidden in the hearts of His redeemed;
In the gloom of shadowed spaces'
Tis a light on lifted faces
From the radiant heavenly places whence it streamed.

Where is the promise of His coming?
It is written in the records of the past,
In the evils unabated,
In the blood-lust still unsated,
In the woes reiterated to the last.

Where is the promise of His coming?
It is shouted by the thunder of the guns,
By the flaming forges burning,
Where the plows to swords are turning,
By the weeping mothers yearning for their sons.

Where is the promise of His coming?
It is flashed around the world with every sun;
Every day's events a token
That God's purpose stands unbroken,
And the thing that He hath spoken shall be done.

Where is the promise of His coming?
All the sentient earth with joy electric hums;
On the waves of air 'tis flowing,
On the winds of heaven blowing,
Sign on sign its surely showing, till He comes.[45]

---

[45] There shall come in the last days scoffers ... saying, Where is the promise of His coming? (2 Peter 3:3,4)

THE WINTER BIRDS

When autumn's flaming torch has set
The hills and vales alight,
Then gather all the feathered clans,
To take their southward flight.
The goldfinch from the thicket flees,
The swallow from the eaves,
His bower in the lilac bush
The slim gray catbird leaves.

From meadow grass, from forest tree,
Go bobolink and thrush,
And over fields and streams and woods
There falls a sudden hush
From all their summer haunts and homes
The Singing Tribes are gone;
Oh, blessings on the winter birds
That bravely linger on!

The flicker shouts across the fields,
The cheery chickadee
Hobnobs with all the sparrow folk,
Those birds of low degree;
The nuthatch makes his daily round,
And hammers on the bark,

Head up, head down, all one to him,
    With many a loud remark.

    I grant they are not musical,
      They sing no tuneful lays,
    But oh, they give a wondrous charm
      To dull and gloomy days.
They break the deathlike calm that broods
    Above the earth's white shroud,
    They twitter in the leafless trees
      Beneath the rainy cloud;

    They drift before the coming storm,
      Half hid in falling snow,
    Like little ghosts of autumns leaves
      Wind-driven to and fro
When come to slow, dark winter morns,
    I hear them at my door,
They chirp their thanks for scattered crumbs,
    And boldly beg for more.

    I love the robin's matin hymn,
      The blackbird's whistle clear,
    The vesper sparrow's dulcet call
      When night's is drawing near,
    The yellow-bird's persistent chant,
      The phoebe's plaintive song;
    But dear, as well, the simple notes
      That cheer the winter long.

    And bright the robin's breast of red
      On some bleak day in spring,
    And gay the oriole's flaming coat,

The bluebird's azure wing;
But fair to me the winter birds
In somber brown and gray,
The little brave and sturdy souls
Who do not go away.

ALPHA AND OMEGA

Christ is the Alpha of our prayers;
We know not how to pray
Save as His Spirit in our hearts
Shall teach us what to say.
Christ is the Omega of prayer,
The Father's great Amen
That rounds our halting periods
To sense beyond our ken.
But in the little space between
He lets us make the links,
And with our slow and stammering speech
Interpret what He thinks.
O First and Last, take Thou the prayers
Of every trusting soul,
And weld them to Thine own desire
To make a perfect whole.
Thou great Beginning of that Word
We cannot speak or spell,
Of the short syllable we lisp
Be Thou the End as well![46]

---

[46] I am Alpha and Omega, the beginning and the ending ... the first and last ... the Amen.
(Revelation 22:13; 3:14)

TOM THUMB YELLOWBIRD

Glint of sunshine and a song:
This is Tom Thumb Yellowbird:
Sure, from such a tiny mite
Louder strain was never heard.
Just a pair of wings and throat,
Midget chorister of glee,
Just two sunbeams and a voice,
Sublimated melody.
True sun-worshipper is he,
Devotee of summertime;
Naught of frost or blight he knows,
Following warmth from clime to clime.
Steeped in sunlight through and through,
Feathered morsel of pure gold,
Greatheart atom, brimming o'er
With the joy he cannot hold.
Gleam of sun, by shadow chased,
Flitting in and out the trees;
Thumb-nail sketch of energy,
Busy as the murmuring bees.
Soul of glad contentment he,
Happy, happy all the day,
Sweetening toil from dawn to dusk
With his tireless roundelay.

AND JESUS

There were six in the room where Death had been;
The little dead maid was one,
Two were the parents with broken hearts
For all they could do was done;
Three were the pitying men who came
To the house where the dead child lay;
And Death was stronger than all of them,
For Death had had his way.

The power of man and the strength of man
Were vain to help or save,
And the mother-love could not restore
The life that once she gave.
But Life had followed the feet of Death
To banish man's despair,
And the child came back from the gates of the grave;
There were six, and Jesus—there.[47]

---

[47] The Raising of Jairus' daughter. (Mark 5:35-42)

THE BABE OF BETHLEHEM

Babe of Bethlehem!
Of whom the angels sang,
For whom their "Peace, Goodwill to men",
Through earth and heaven rang.
To whom the shepherds knelt,
To whom the wise men came
With precious gifts from lands afar,
Led by the star aflame.

O Babe of Bethlehem!
Still looks the world to Thee
From whom the Kings of Earth
Hold crowns and throne in fee;
Still do the wise men bring
Their science and their art
And own their highest wisdom yet
Is but of Thee a part.

Still do the humble come,
Leaving their toil a while,
To where Thy presence is revealed,
To where Thy face doth smile.
O Babe of Bethlehem!
All things to all Thou art;

Thou knowest every need
Of every human heart.

The Shepherd Thou who leads at eve
His flock into the fold,
The Potter who with skillful hand
Our mortal day doth mold,
In sorrow or in joy,
A sympathizing Friend,
A brother kind and true,
Who loves us to the end;

The Jesus who upon the Cross
From sin His people saves,
The Christ who fills with light and hope
The darkness of our graves.
Thee do we still adore,
To Thee our praises rise;
The Living Water Thou,
The Bread that satisfies.

To thee for peace we turn,
From Thee our strength doth spring,
In Thee our rest we find,
To Thee our burdens bring;
With whom our life is hid,
By whom our life is given,
The Truth amid a world of dreams,
The Way that leads to Heaven;

To Thee alone we come
Who hast the words of life,
Through Thee alone we hope

For victory in the strife;
By Thee our work is crowned,
Through Thee our trust we keep,
And by Thy grace, when day is done,
In Thee we fall asleep.

BARABBAS' SUBSTITUTE

What didst thou think upon that day,
Barabbas malefactor vile,
Awaiting agony and death
In that short while,
When to thy prison door one came
And said, "Barabbas, thou art free;
Another man will take thy place
And die for thee"?

With awe and trembling wonder filled,
Thou must have followed to the place
Where He was nailed upon thy cross,
To see His face;
Thou must have marked thy fellow thief,
And listened to his pleading cry,
And heard the confident, clear voice
That made reply.

Thou must have owned thy lasting debt
To Him whose death for thee sufficed,
And said, "This man is more than man;
"This is the Christ."
Thou must have felt thy hardened heart
With love and gratitude o'erflow

To Him who bore thy punishment,
And let thee go.

And shall my own heart love Him less?
For, as He died that day for thee,
Barabbas, murdered and thief,
And set thee free,
So, when my guilty soul deserved
The law's extreme penalty,
He died, my sinless Substitute,
Instead of me.[48]

---

[48] And Pilate released Barabbas ... and delivered Jesus ... to be crucified. (Mark 15:15)

THE PHOEBE BIRD

When springtime days are bright and fair
And skies are blue and shining,
A lonely tittle bachelor
Goes grieving and repining;
Among the budding orchard trees,
From dawn to dark he's calling,
Athwart the robins' cheery tones
His plaintive accents falling—
Phoe-be— Phoe-be —where's Phoe-be?"

O cruel must the maiden be
To leave him thus despairing,
The while she loiters on the road
For his distress uncaring!
When other birds are glad and gay
And blithely they are singing,
He still repeats his pleading cry
As here and there he's winging—
"Phoe-be — Phoe-be —come, Phoe-be!"

He has no heart his home to plan—
That has nest of dainty beauty—
Till she has come his toil to share
In wifely love and duty.

So all the day this faithful swain
His loneliness is voicing:
O Phoe-be, come, and end his plaint,
And he shall! sing, rejoicing,
" Phoe-be — Phoe-be —here's Phoe-be!"

FAITH AND SIGHT

At even, we shall know that the Lord hath brought us out;
Though the darkness deepen round us, we shall feel no fear or doubt,
For the fiery pillar shields us, and its burning is our light,
And we rest beneath its shadow while the evening brings the night.
We shall know - for now we can trust Him who hath led us all the way;
Who hath ransomed and redeemed us, who hath been our staff and stay;
Who hath made a path before us through the desert and the sea.
To the Lord who sought and saved us, evermore our praise shall be.
At even we shall know; but at morning we shall see,
When our hope is lost in vision and our faith in victory;
We shall sup with Him at even, when the rose of sunset dies;
Ere the lurid morning cometh, we shall see the Star arise.
He shall keep us safely hidden while His judgments shake the world,
While His word shall smite the nations, into wreck and ruin hurled;
We shall see the opened heavens, we shall follow in His train,
We shall come with Him in triumph when He comes to earth to reign.
Glory! Glory! His glory! His the kingdom! His the power!
When the Sun shall break in splendor through the clouds that darkly lower,
We shall see it, we shall share it; let this hope our comfort be—
As we know Him at the even, in the morning we shall see.[49]

---

[49] At even, ye shall know that the Lord hath brought you out from the land of Egypt; and in the morning ye shall see the glory of the Lord. (Exodus 16:6,7)

A FRIEND'S FIRST BIRTHDAY IN HEAVEN

We gave thee gifts when thou wert here—
Bright flowers that faded with the day,
And dainty fineries to wear,
And books to read, and games to play;
But now—what shall we bring thee now?
What can we give thee where thou art?

Gone from us to that larger life,
What dost thou lack, dear heart, sweet heart?
The joy of God is in thy soul,
His peace upon thy forehead lies,
And 'round thy feet forever bloom
The fadeless flowers of paradise.

What can we bring but love that grieves
And memories that sadly cling
'Round the dear spot where thou didst dwell,
And sorrowing hope with broken wing?
Nay, couldst thou speak, wouldst thou not say:—
"Are these the gifts that honor me?

Bring love that triumphs over death
And links me still to earth and thee;
And hope that weeps not at the grave,

But looks beyond the empty tomb;
And faith that sees me waiting here,
And smiling on thee through the gloom.

"And bring thy memories if thou wilt,
Dear memories of the happy past,
But know, the present's lonely way
Leads on to where we meet at last;
And find a balm for others' woe
E'en in thine own Gethsemane;

Learn there the comfort to bestow
Wherewith the Father comforts thee.
"So shalt thou share my heaven with me,
So shalt thou know the joy I feel,
So shalt thou see, o'er grief and tears,
The glory of the rainbow steal;
So shall the love that sent the cross
Give peace beneath the chast'ning rod.

THE GATES OF THE COURT

It is through the gates of thanksgiving
That we enter the courts of praise;
Our thanks for the little bounties
That compass us all our days
Shall bring us to greater blessings,
And lead us to larger ways.

O Lord of the manifold mercies,
As we number them one by one,
From the least of Thy loving kindness
To the uttermost gift of Thy Son,
Lead us on from our selfish gladness
To the marvellous things Thou hast done.

As we offer our small rejoicing
For the love that surrounds our days,
All the wonderful works of Thy goodness
Shall open before our gaze;
Through the gates of our narrow thanksgiving
We shall enter Thy courts of praise.[50]

---

[50] Enter into His gates with thanksgiving, and into His courts with praise. (Psalm 10:4)

DO THOU

Do Thou for me, God, my God;
Helpless, I appeal to Thee;
What is best I cannot tell,
What is right I cannot see.
Blind, I dread to stand or go,
And I fear to lose the way,
For I know not what to do
And I know not how to pray.
Hear my cry: "Do Thou for me,
I can trust it all with Thee."

Fight Thou for me, God, my God;
How shall I my foes withstand?
I should only fail and yield;
Take the battle in Thy hand.
Thou my Rock, my Strength, my Shield.
Lo, I flee to Thee for aid;
Weak, so weak, but be my strength
Perfect through that weakness made.
Hear my cry: "Fight Thou for me—
More than conqueror I shall be."

Live Thou for me, God, my God;
Come Thou and abide in me,

That my sinful self my die,
Daily my crucified with Thee.
Think my thoughts and speak my words,
Move my lips, my hands, my feet,
Till Thou art unveiled in me
And Thine image is complete.
Hear my cry: "Live Thou for me,
Thus alone I live for Thee."

DO THEY REMEMBER?

How do they mark the passing years
Those dwellers in the higher sphere?
How do they count the seasons there,
Where Time is not and shall not be,
And through the bright Eternity
They only grow more young and fair?
What glorious fete-days do they keep
While here with us the slow years creep?
And do they oft make holiday
As when they walked our darker way?

I fancy that at Christmas time
The angel-messengers repeat
The story of the Saviour's birth,
While faintly, from some Christmas chime,
An answering cadence, clear and sweet,
Floats upward from the star'lit Earth;
And choiring seraphim renew
The song of glory and a peace,
The song the Bethlehem shepherds knew,
Whose echoes never wholly cease.

And on each radiant Easter dawn
The hosts redeemed may softlier sing,

That so our feebler notes of praise,
In worship of our Risen King,
May add a deeper tone of joy
To mingle with their glad refrain.
Earth's minor making sweeter still
The music of the heavenly strain.

But oh! these frailer mortal ties;
Do friends look down with tender eyes,
Upon our wistful hearts that hold
In memory dear some day of old,
Ere Earth was emptied of their smile
And life was ravished of their face?
And do they bear in mind the while
The birthdays and the marriage-days
That star our calendars in red?
Is there remembrance with the dead?

For us, in lieu of clasp and kiss
Our love can compass only this;
To heap the low green mound with flow'rs.
There is no more that we can do,
They need not any gift of ours;
But it were not so hard to bear
These days that they no longer share,
If we could know that somewhere, they,
Still one with us, keep holiday,
And through the years remember, too.

BEATING ME HOME

Through the shady lane, ere the sun had set,
We strolled together, my boy and I;
Far above our heads, where the treetops met
And the blue sky shone through a lacy net,
The birds were singing a lullaby.

And the small boy chattered, as small boys can
Of all he meant to do and be;
How he'd grow and grow to a great big man–
And the short arms stretched to their utmost span–
And work his hardest, and all for me.

At the end of the lane he stayed his feet,
With wistful eyes on the way that led
From the sleepy calm of the village street
To the city's noise and the city's heat;
"Oh, why do we never go there?" he said.

So I answered again the old demand,
The road was dusty and hard and long;
And I gathered closer the little hand,
For I fain would keep him in childhood's land,
Untouched by sorrow and pain and wrong.

Then, his quest forgotten in eager play,
He turned to the home lane, cool and green,
He loosed my hand as he sped away
And I heard him calling me, clear and gay,
When swaying branches had dropped between.

Now his words are echoing o'er and o'er,
Through my empty heart and the empty air:-
"Mother dear, I'm beating you home once more
I'll go ahead and open the door,
Just follow me show and you'll find me there."

Oh, the Home he has reached is safe and sweet,
And slow my walk through a long, long lane
As I follow the prints of his flying feet,
And lest for his laughter mine ears to greet,
Follow and listen, and not in vain.

I have done forever with all my fears;
No care shall sadden his joyous song,
And his eyes shall never be dimmed by tears,
For the child heart beats through the endless years
Untouched by sorrow and pain and wrong.

And I know, though the silence hurts me sore
And still to my longing his voice is dumb,
He has only "beaten me home" once more,
He has "gone ahead to open the door,"
And there he's waiting for me to come.

AT THE CROSS OF JESUS

There is love at the cross of Jesus, an everlasting love
That could leave the courts of heaven and the glory of God above,
That could come to a world of evil for the sake of the sinners lost,
That could drain the cup of anguish and never count the cost.

There is light at the cross of Jesus, though dark is the world around;
It was there He opened heaven, and the way to God was found;
It was there the tempest gathered and broke on His thorn-crowned head,
When He bore our stripes and sorrows, and suffered in our stead.

There is peace at the cross of Jesus, where God was reconciled,
Where we know our sins forgiven and hear Him say, "My child";
Where He bore the world's transgressions and all our debt was paid;
Where the weight of the Father's anger on His tender heart was laid.

There is life at the cross of Jesus, where the victory was won,
Where sin and death were conquered by the sin-less, deathless One;
O grave, where is thy triumph? O death, where is thy sting?
For the Lord of life and glory passed through thy gates a King!

THE ROBIN'S NOTE

Blithe bird of the morning, that heralds the dawn,
How joyous the sound of his carolling free;
Ere the first gleam of silver has brightened the cast
He sings that the night and the darkness shall flee,
And a memory sweet and a prophecy sure
Are mingled in one in that jubilant strain—
Grief and gladness long past, grief and gladness to come —
Till my heart swells in answer with joy and with pain.
"Be cheery, my dearie, day's coming, night's gone;
Far up in the treetop I welcome the dawn.
There's a nestful of love and all heaven above,
No clouds in the blue but the sun can shine through.
So I sing all the day under bright skies or gray;
There's naught to be sad for and much to be glad for;
Be cheery, my dearie, keep singing alway."

Dear singer of sunset, I hear him at eve,
When still is the blackbird and silent the thrush;
For a bliss bubbles over within his full heart
Not even the coming of twilight can hush.
He sings in the sunshine and sings in the rain
With a faith in the future no storm cloud can dim;
"In all things give thanks,"—he obeys the command,
For shadow and sun seem alike unto him.

"Be cheery, my dearie, look up and be glad;
Though the weather be dreary, oh, never be sad!
Let it rain if it will; though the wind may be chill,
Over gray skies are blue, and the sun will shine through.
So I sing just as clear when the day's dark and dearer;
There's much to be glad for and naught to be sad for;
Be cheery, my dearie, keep singing alway."

ALL THE DAYS

Yea, I am with thee when there falls no shadow
Across the golden glory of the day,
And I am with thee when the storm-clouds gather,
Dimming the brightness of the onward day;
In days of loss, and loneliness and sorrow,
Of care and weariness and fretting pain,
In days of weakness and of deep depression,
Of futile effort when thy life seems vain;
When youth has fled and Death has put far from thee
Lover and friend who made the journey sweet,
When Age has come with slowly failing powers,
And the dark valley waits thy faltering feet;
When courage fails thee for the unknown future;
And the heart sinks beneath its weight of fears;
Still I am with thee - Strength and Best and Comfort,
Thy Counsellor through all Earth's changing years.
Whatever goes, whatever stays,
Lo, I am with thee all the days.

THE YEARS OF HIS RIGHT HAND

"I have covered there in the shadow of mine hand" (Isaiah 51:16)
I remember the years of His hand's deep shadow-
The sun was darkened, the stars were veiled,
The glory of life was a fading flower,
And mirth was over and music failed;
But in that shade I was safely hidden,
From wind and tempest I knew release,
And for the old, new songs were given,
My heart learned patience, my soul found peace.

"I will uphold thee with the right hand of my righteousness" (Isaiah 41:10)
I remember the years of His hand's upholding-
Its help how mighty, its clasp how strange;
Almost I slipped when my feet were sliding,
Almost I fell when the way was long;
But never once did His strength forsake me,
And when I leaned on His wondrous might,
On wings I mounted, I ran unwearied,
I walked unfainting, by day or night.

"Thou shalt remember all the way which
the Lord thy God led thee" (Deuteronomy 8:2)
I remember the years of His hand's sure leading-
How safe His guidance, His ways how wise,

Often my thoughts and my heart would wander,
My feet would follow my straying eyes;
But never once did His patience fail me,
And through it all did His love restrain,
And when I followed where He would lead me,
How all the way and the end grew plain.

"I have graven thee upon the palms of my hands" (Isaiah 49:16)
I remember the years of His hand's safe keeping–
When danger threatened or sin beset,
When, the rudder fallen from nerveless fingers,
My life-bark drifted where wild seas met;
But through it all did His power keep me,
And now I know, when my foes assail,
Strong to deliver, He waits to succor,
And prays for me lest my faith should fail.

***"The Lord ... will hear ... from His holy heaven with the
saving strength of His right hand" (Psalm 20:6)***
Oh, I know that my name on Thy palms is graven,
I remember the years of Thy hand, Most High!
How it has sheltered and held and guided
"Neath clouded heaven or open sky;
I lean on Thine arm and Thy hand upholds me,
Its power protects and its strength defends;
Still it shall hide me and keep and lead me
Till Home is reached and the journey ends.[51]

---

[51] I will remember the years of the right hand of the Most High. (Psalm 77:10)

WHEN CHRIST WAITS

What a wonderful thing is this
That man may choose as he will
To open the door and let Christ in,
Or make Him wait at the still!

The sovereign Lord of the universe,
Courteous, stands and knocks;
He will not batter the shut door down,
Nor break the bolts and locks.

For man has the power of choice,
He can lift the latch if he will;
There is no knob on the outer side,
And the Lord Christ waits at the still.

He patiently knocks and patiently waits
For man to open the door;
Beware the day when His patience ends,
And the pierced Hand knocks no more![52]

---

[52] If any man ... open the door, I will come in. (Revelation 3:20)

THE WAY TO HEAVEN

Just "turn to the right, and keep straight on,"
And you cannot miss the way,
"Is it rough?" you ask; oh, yes sometimes;
But it's rougher if you stray.

For to all who travel the one sure road
There's a perfect Guide-book given;
But there's no map shown of the lands around;
It's only the way to heaven.

So, when you have started, keep straight on,
Turn neither to left nor right,
For danger lurks on either side
Though the signals all burn "white";

There are hands that beckon and lips that call,
And the shady lanes look sweet;
But they hold a lure for the wavering heart
And a snare for the wandering feet.

The Lord of the land to which we go
Has servants many and true,
And the only road to their heavenly home
Is the one you are walking to;

And never yet was the way so hard,
Or the night so dark and long,
But some one offered a helping hand
And some one started a song.

So "turn to the right, and keep straight on,"
And a guide-book will be given.
There's no map shown of the lands around,
But it tells the way to heaven.[53]

---

[53] Ask ... where is the good way, and walk therein. (Jeremiah 6:16)

THE WATER LILY'S STORY

When first I woke to life,
Deep down in the river's bed,
I could not breathe for the stifling ooze
And the blackness over my head.
In darkness I longed for the light,
Prisoned, I yearned to be free,
In dreams I pined for the sky and wind,
For star and bird and tree;
And I said: "I will rise to that upper air,
And the life that draweth me."
The twining weeds of the water-world
Reached out and held me fast;
The little reeds wove a tangled net
To catch me as I passed;
The creeping things of mire and mud
Beckoned and bade me stay;
In the treacherous current, swift and strong,
I felt my weak stem away;
But through them, over them, past them all,
I took my upward way.
Till, while, white,
Brimmed with sunshine and steeped in light,
I lifted up my fragrant cup-
Bloom of the daytime and star of the night-

In rapture I gazed at the heavens blue
And knew that all my dreams were true.
And pure and fair my white leaves bear
Never a trace of slime and mold,
And the crawling things of the under-world
Have left to taint on my heart of gold.
In peace I rest on the river's breast,
And living, I love, and, loving, live,
And breathing deep of that upper air,
My life to the world in sweetness give.
In the stifling air of the lower world,
Oh, Soul, do you dream, as I,
Of the pure, clear light and the sunshine's gold,
And the blue of the open sky?
Rise from your dreaming and lift your head
From the death-in-life of the clinging clay,
And, spurning every base desire,
Mounting higher and yet higher,
Hold on your upward way.
Till, pure and white,
Filled with glory and steeped in light,
No trace of the soil from whence it springs
Staining the Soul's expanding wings,
You too shall see the arching heaven's blue
And find that all your dreams are true.
You shall eat of joy as your daily bread,
Through love you shall learn and by loving live;
You shall drink of life at the fountain head,
And that life to the world in sweetness give.

THE TWO BOOKS

There are two books in the archives of heaven
Where I am fain that my name shall be graven.
One is Jehovah's great Book of Remembrance
Of those who have feared Him and thought on His name,
Where, on the white pages spread open before Him,
Is written His glorious roster of fame.
And when I have reached the bright portals of glory,
And past is the suffering, past is the strife,
I know through the merits of Jesus my Saviour
I'll find my name there in the Lamb's Book of Life.
The books of the world may forever disdain it;
No records of earthland may ever contain it;
But these are the books in the archives of heaven
Wherein I am fain that my name shall be graven.[54] [55]

---

[54] And a book of remembrance was written before him. (Malachi 3:16)

[55] They which are written in the Lamb's book of life. (Revelation 21:27)

WHEN THE BIRDS BUILD

Hear the chorus that the birds are singing:
Oh, the skies are blue!
From the Sunny South their fight now winging;
Oh, the skies are blue!
To begin again their happy, happy questing
Till they find a place that suits them for their nesting;
Elm-tree, chestnut, maple, there's no telling—
Oh, the skies are blue!
Where they'll choose to build their airy dwelling;
Oh, the skies are blue!
Apple-trees are white and pink and growing pinker,
Every honey-bee has turned a drinker,
Oh, the skies are blue!

Blackbird, oriole,—a saucy fellow!
Oh, the skies are blue!—
In his dashing suit of black and yellow;
Oh, the skies are blue!
Wren and swallow and the crimson-breasted robin,
Wings a-flutter and their little heads a-bobbin',
Sticks and straw from every corner looting,
Oh, the skies are blue!
Send from tree to tree their cheery fluting,
Oh, the skies are blue!

Every throat, from bobolink to tiny linnet,
Bubbling over with the music in it;
Oh, the skies are blue!

THE SEASHELL

Here let it lie, beside its ancient home,
Nor bear it far away from all it knows,
From all it loves, remembers and desires;
Fit toy for Aphrodite, ere she rose.

From cradle-rockings of the summer seas
To be the joy and solace of the earth.
So leave it here; the tide may draw it back
To those translucent depths that gave it birth.

What music murmurous yet fills its heart,
What haunting fragments of lost melodies,
What lovely half-forgotten minor strains,
What crashing chords and stormy symphonies.

What rippling lullabies in still lagoons,
What flooding harmonies of winds and waves,
What mournful requiems on coral reefs,
What organ anthems o'er unquiet graves.

Could we but know what memories it keeps!
Perchance upon a far-off, golden morn
It saw the sportive Nereids at play,
And heard same Triton blow his wreathed horn.

Perchance it heard the clash of smitten shields
Half drown the thunder shout of Cyrus' horde,
"Thalassa!" and "Thalassa!" ringing down
The slope o'er which the great Ten Thousand poured.

Perchance it saw the Argonaut's brave prows
Turn seaward on their argent questing long:
Perchance it watched Ulysses at the mast,
Self-bound, drift past the sirens' luring song:

Perchance it heard the wrathful tempest roar
That whelmed Leander in its seething tide,
And saw the flickering torchlight paint the wave
That beat against the rocks where Hero died.

So, leave it here upon the wave-wet sand,
Among the seaweed and the flying foam,
That soon the ebbing tide may draw it back
And bear it downward to its ancient home.

MORNING GLORIES

Little bits of bloom celestial
On the earth reborn,
Pink and purple, snow and azure,
Each new day adorn;
Little chalices of beauty,
Trumpets of delight,
Cups of joy distilled in darkness
From the dews of night.
Fragile beauty, fleeting glory.
Short the hour that's given;
Yet each night and morning finds them
So much nearer heaven;
Though the blossoms droop and wither,
Still the clinging vine
Round each bar that lifts it higher
Eagerly will twine;
Striving, reaching, grasping, holding,
Upward, o'er and o'er,
So the heavenly morning-glories
Seek their home once more.
Let our hearts thus greet Each morning,
Joyous as the day;
Let our souls thus climb to heaven
From the earth away.

IN THE BEGINNING

The lights of the city gleam and glow
In the misty purple dusk,
Bursting out of the grimy globes
Like tropical fruits from the husk:
A myriad sparkling orbs of light,—
Violet, golden, scarlet, white, —
Blazing up at the stars of night.
But the light was not in the globes,
Man's hand has led it there,
His power, his thought, the wonder wrought,
Captured and chained the flare;
And the light obeys his will,
The mind of man and his skill.

But back of the light is the power house,
Where the great wheels tireless turn,
Where the pulleys lift and the gearings shift,
And the rearing fires burn.
And back of the power the mine,
Where the toiling slaves of the Lamp
Burrow like moles in the black pit-holes
In the dust and the deadly damp.

And back of the mine are the buried trees

Where the strong winds laid them low,
Charred by the fires of centuries,
Smoldering deep and slow;
The days of the Lord are a thousand years,
The eves and the morns of the circling spheres,
And a thousand thousand lingering days
Passed over the trees and the hidden blaze.

THE CRAG OF THE CROSS

Beside the bleak coast of the Northland,
Where winds with the tempests keep tryst,
Amid a wild welter of waters,
An island looms out of the mist;
Forever the high tides of Fundy
Sweep past with a rush and a roar,
Forever the gulls cry their warning
When fog wreathes the desolate shore;

Above the gray billows the cliffs frown,
Above the grim cliffs bends the sky,
And clear against cliff-side and heavens
The Crag of the Cross rises high.
Of old hath He laid its foundations
Who holdeth the sea in His hand,
Who weigheth its waters by measure
And setteth their bounds by the sand;

And slowly His craftsmen have carved it,
—the frost and the storm and the wave—
Rough-hewn from the rock everlasting
Where sons their annals might grave.
Long, long ere o'er Bethlehem's manger
The Star shed its radiant light,

And long ere on: Calvary's summit
The noonday was shrouded in night;

While kingdoms and nations had risen
And played their brief parts for a day,
And countless new creeds and old systems
Had flourished and passed to decay;
While oracles lapsed into silence
And prophets grew weary and dumb,
The Cross, through the centuries waiting,
Was pledge of a faith yet to come.

And never the surf overwhelms it
And never the surges o'erflow
Though still through the storm and the sunshine
The treacherous tides come and go;
They toss, but they may not pass over;
They roar, but they shall not prevail,
And day after day they are baffled
And night after night they shall fail;

Forever in vain is their striving
To foil the decree He hath made:
"Thus far shalt thou come but no farther,
And here shall thy proud waves be stayed,"
Their force and their arts all defying,
The Crag every onset shall breast,
And come they in peace or in anger,
At the foot of the cross they must rest.

In summer, like shimmering opals,
The dawn-tinted waters will sleep
Till comes the mysterious signal

And stealthily landward they creep;
With soft sighing whispers beguiling
They playfully break on the beach,
With musical rippling and plashing
The sweet sing'ing voices beach.

Like sycophants fawning and coaxing,
Caressing and dimpling in glee;
But ever the Cross rises silent,
Majestic, unmoved by their plea.
And winter's black hordes charge as vainly,
Hurled forward with thunderous shocks,
With crash of relentless battalions
And rending and grinding of rocks;

Urged on by the lash of the storm-wind
And heedless of all in their path,
They batter the outlying ridges
With hissing white torrents of wrath.
Till, raging in impotent fury,
Before the great Crag they retreat,
And, beaten to sullen submission,
Come crouching again at its feet.

Then, while the last sob of the tempest
Swells faint from the darkening west,
In billows all jade in the hollow
And burnished to gold on the crest,
Up out of the seas of the Tropics
The moon leads her glittering host—
The ranks of her silver-clad cohorts—
To fling them once more on the coast.

The half-sunken ledges are covered,
The shallows are flooded and filled,
Afar in the echoing caverns
The deep organ-murmurs are stilled;
Above the heaped rocks of the shore-line
The foam-whitened breakers shall toss,
Till over the wide waste of waters
There rises naught else but the Cross.

So sink man's achievements and triumphs
Beneath the gray flood of the years,
So vanish the works of his wisdom,
The schools and the temples he rears.
So cease both his dream and his doing,
So perish his purpose and thought,
So pass all his pride and his power
And all that his power hath wrought;

His tombs and his towers are shattered
And buried in slow-drifting sand,
His columns of victory fallen,
Laid low by Time's leveling hand.
His cities are dust-heaps and ruins
In deserts untrodden and lone,
Their splendor long lost and forgotten,
Their names and their places unknown.

He writes on a shore that already
Is wet with the oncoming spray,
Where swift-flowing tides shall efface it
And blot out his records for aye;
He spendeth his life as a shadow
And only its passing is sure —

But through all the ages unchanging,
The Cross and its glory endure.[56]

---

[56] The Crag of the Cross is a natural formation on the Island of Manan, in the
Bay of Fundy.

THE CAMP FIRE

Cheerily crackles the morning fire,
While the red flashes mount higher and higher;
Twisting and bending, smoke wreaths ascending,
Earth sounds and air sounds in harmony blending:
Bright through the tree tops the sunlight is falling,
Joy is awaking! A new day is breaking!
Rise to its labors, your slumbers forsaking:
Heap on the fagots, stir the blaze higher,
Cheerily, cosily, crackles the fire.
Good morning!

Dreamily flickers the evening fire
While the dusk shadows creep higher and higher,
Daylight is ending, quiet's descending,
Earth sounds and air sounds in peacefulness blending:
Dim through the tree tops the starlight is falling,
Soft in the silence a drowsy bird's calling:
Sleepily winking, stealthily blinking,
All the red coals into ashes are sinking.
Cover the embers lest it burn higher, —
Dreamily, drowsily smoulders the fire.
Good night!

WHILE THE BRIDEGROOM TARRIES

"Where tarry the wheels of Thy chariot, Jesus our lord?"
"Close at hand, though unseen, I am waiting
To speak the great word
That calls you from sin and from sorrow
To reign at My side;
With groanings that cannot be uttered
I yearn for My bride,
For the sons I have brought to salvation
At Calvary's cost,
For the souls I have brought from destruction,
That none may be lost.
I wait a one waits for the morning,
For dawn to arise;
No slumber shall visit Mine eyelids,
No sleep close mine eyes,
Till the heritage promised aforetime
I claim for My own,
Till the kingdoms of earth are My kingdom
And I mount My throne."

"Yet I tarry" - "Oh, why dost Thou tarry,
Thou long-promised King,
When the world is awaiting Thy coming,
Redemption to bring?"

"I wait till My church is completed,
The full number sealed,
That no precious sheaf may be left
In the wide harvest field.
When the reapers go forth with their sickles
To garner the wheat;
That no single grain may be burnt
In the flame of My feet,
When the long day of grace shall be ended,
And judgment begun;
And I came in the clouds of heavens,
And shine like the sun.
I am waiting for you, oh My saved ones!
For you to go forth
To the East and the West with My message,
The south and the North.
Go ye, that I come the more quickly,
I listen to hear
My good news of joy and salvation
Fall sweet in My ear.
I gave it in trust for your telling;
Still Faithful and True,
I wait with long suffering patience
With you, and for you;
I had not forgotten My promise,
It is you who are late;
Must I tarry much longer, Beloved?
Oh, hasten, I wait!"[57] [58]

---

[57] The Lord is not slack concerning His promise ... but is long suffering to usward, not willing that any should perish, but that all should come to repentance. (2 Peter 3:9)

[58] O my dove, that art in the clefts of the rock ... let me see Thy countenance, let me hear thy voice. (Song of Songs 2:14)

THE BRIDGE BUILDERS

Oh, never the land of their birth can hold them!
The wastes untrodden shall call them far,
Where winds of an alien clime enfold them,
Lone 'neath the light of a stranger star.
Earth makes them free of her secret places,
And one with her ageless solitudes;
The heirs are they of her high, still spaces,
Friends of the forest, and wards of the woods.

Their foes are the swamp, the racing river,
Fathomless quicksand and jungle's breath,
The icy chill and the wasting fever,
Imminent danger and waiting death;
But theirs the courage to face disaster,
The stubborn patience, the cunning skill;
The forces of nature they meet and master,
Tame and bend to their utmost will.

Where the hush of creation rests unbroken
Their shrieking whistles that calm shall break;
Where never the voice of man hath spoken
Their drills and hammers the echoes wake.
At their commandment the rocks are riven,
The mountains move and the seas are stayed,

Where wild beasts hunted their stakes are driven,
Where eagles nested their trail is made.

With chain and compass and line and plummet
They gauge and measure and bound their dream:
They pierce the peak and they scale the summit,
Harness the torrent and hale the stream:
Where plunging cataracts fall in thunder
Their airy webs o'er the void are hung:
Where whirlpools whiten, the girders under,
Their piers are fixed and their trestles flung.

They level the hull and they fill the hollow
To make a road for the men who roam,
Smooth and straight for the feet that follow,
Seeking for pleasure or gold or home.
Though hidden treasure their picks uncover,
They leave and lose it and stall press on;
In the van of progress their armies hover,
Here today, and tomorrow gone.

Before them the silence of desolation,
Waterless desert and treeless plain;
Behind them the tread of a marching nation,
Roaring cities and leagues of grain.
The wilderness yields to their slow persistence,
The reef and the tundra their word await;
The peaceful victors of space and distance,
The mighty masters of time and fate!

LULLABY OF RAIN

Through the sultry city daylight I had toiled with throbbing head,
But at night, though spent and weary, slumber from my working fled;
Still before my aching vision lines of figures came and went,
Ghosts of those long hours of labor and the day's imprisonment,
Only glare and tumult entered through the window opened wide,
Naught of freshness e'er could reach me from the surging human tide;
Then a muttered growl of thunder and the lightning's far off flare,
And a sudden breath of coolness in the hot and murky air;
There's a patter on the shingles and a tap against the pane;
Oh, the orchestra is tuning for the Lullaby of Rain!
Now the spell it weaves about me wraps me in its mesh of dreams
Till reality is blended with the thing that only seems,
And my sigh of soft contentment wafts my thought, like homing dove,
Straight on swift, unerring pinion to a little house I love,
Far away from city pavements, never jangling sound it hears,
Watchers of the dawns and sunsets through the peaceful passing years;
When the twilight calm enfolds it and the purple mists arise,
Oh, a whispered benediction falls the hush of even-tide,
Changeless through the changing seasons doth my House of Memories bide.

I can hear the water running from the overhanging eaves,
And a liquid, lisping trickle from the elm-tree's drooping leaves,
There's a clatter on the shingles and a splash against the pane,
Oh, I know the blessed prelude to the Lullaby of Rain!

Sweeter than the censer's fragrance is the orchard's rosy bloom,
Spicy odors floating upward to that low-ceiled attic room;
Dim against the outer blackness gleams the window's open space,
And the faint, elusive earth-scents, drifting through it, cool my face.
I can smell the fresh wet lilacs from the bush beside the door,
And the quick tears burn the eyelids - I shall enter their no more.
I can hear the sleepy twitter of a bird's note from the trees,
And the meadow-brook's hoarse murmur, borne upon the rising breeze;
There's a choked and chuckling gurgle from the overflowing eaves,
And a drip! drip! drip *staccato* from the soaked and streaming leaves,
Then a rush along the shingles and a dash against the pane,
Oh, a hundred voices mingle in the Lullaby of Rain!
Now the single sounds are merging in a long, *crescendo* roar
That shall drown all lesser noises in its steady pelting pour;
Hence you phantoms of old labour! You shall haunt me now in vain,
As I drift away to dreamland to the Lullaby of Rain.

IN HIM

"We dwell in Him," oh, everlasting Home,
Imperishable House not made with hands!
When all the world has melted as a dream,
Eternal in the heav'ns this dwelling stands.[59]

---

[59] We know that we dwell in Him. (1 John 4:13)

BY THE WAY

Go with me Master, by the way,
Make every day a walk with Thee,
New glory shall the sunshine gain,
And all the clouds shall lightened be.
Go with me on life's dusty road
And help me bear the weary load.

Talk with me, Master, by the way
The voices of the world recede,
The shadows darken o'er the land,
How poor I am, how great my need,
Speak to my heart disquieted,
Till it shall lose its fear and dread.

Bide with me, Master, all the way
Though to my blinded eyes unknown
So shall I feel a Presence near
Where I had thought I walked alone.
And when, far spent, the days decline,
Break Thou the bread, dear Guest of mine![60]

---

[60] Did not our hearts burn within us, while he talked with us by the way? (Luke 24:32)

THE SENTINEL

The morning is the gate of day
But ere you enter there,
See that you set, to guard it well,
The sentinel of prayer.
So shall your steps God's grace attend
But nothing else pass through
Save what can give the countersign:
"The Father's Will for you."

When you have reached the end of day
Where night and sleep await,
Set there the sentinel again
To bar the evening's gate.
So shall no fear disturb your rest,
No danger and no care,
For only peace and pardon pass
The watchful guard of prayer.

UNTO THE LEAST OF THESE

What would you do for Jesus?
If Jesus were here today?
Hungry and thirsty and weary
Fainting beside the way?
What would you give for His comfort?
What would you do for his ease?
Hear now His voice entreating
"Will you not do it for these?"
Cruellest mockings and scourgings
These for His name they have borne,
Walking His sorrowful pathway,
Wearing His crown of thorn;
Driven from home and from country,
Outcast, forsaken and lone,
What would you do for his brethren?
What will you do for your own?
Out of peace and your plenty,
Out of your comfort and ease,
All you would do for Jesus
He would have you do for these.[61]

---

[61] All ye are brethren. (Matthew 23:8)

THE GREATEST BLESSING

Day after day He showers us with blessings
Night after night His bounty overflows.
Joy unto joy His boundless love is adding,
Gift unto gift His faithfulness bestows.

Behind us all the past with good is studded,
Star-points of light in memory's darkening skies.
And faring onwards to an unknown future,
Before us still new constellations rise.

But when the sun springs forth in radiant splendour
And floods the world with glory and with light,
How swift the shadows flee! How melts the darkness!
How pale the stars that seemed so fair and bright!

So when we let Him in - the Life Abundant -
Fling wide the doors and drop the hindering bars,
He comes, the Giver, all His gifts transcending,
As doth the sun the rushlights of the stars.

HE IS OUR PEACE

The loving heart of Jesus was broken for my peace,
The tender hands of Jesus were pierced for my release.
This is the sure foundation on which my faith is built,
This is the one salvation from sin, its power and guilt.
This is the only glory my clouded life can claim,
Redemption's wondrous story of love and death and shame,
This my assurance voicing, and this my only plea,
My song and my rejoicing forevermore shall be.
The broken heart of Jesus alone could save from sin;
The wounded hands of Jesus alone my peace could win.

I SHALL YET PRAISE HIM

I shall yet praise him - though blossoms have withered,
Empty the fold is and barren the field,
All the promise of harvest has vanished,
Fig tree an olive have failed in their yield.
I shall yet praise him - though now the mists shroud me,
Though through the darkness there shineth no star
Though long delayed be the word of his counsel,
And to all seeming He hideth afar.
I shall yet praise him for victory given;
Though fierce the sifting, His prayer cannot fail;
Till the fourth watch He may leave me in darkness;
Then clouds shall lift and the light shall prevail.
I shall yet praise him who knoweth my pathway,
For all His leading through desert and sea,
For the sure promise that standeth forever,
For all his purpose fulfilled unto me.
I shall yet praise him - mute mouth filled with laughter,
Silent lips opened and tongue tuned to song;
Surely praise waiteth; joy, sown for my reaping,
Cometh to harvest, though lingering long. [62]

---

[62] Why art thou cast down, O my soul? and why art thou disquieted in me? hope thou in God: for
I shall yet praise him for the help of his countenance. (Psalm 42:5)

MORE FROM ANNIE JOHNSON FLINT

The Making of The Beautiful - The Life Story of Annie Johnson Flint

Annie Johnson Flint was born in New Jersey, USA on Christmas Eve in 1866, now over 150 years ago. Crippled with arthritis throughout her life, hers was a difficult journey to glory - but, perhaps similar to Fanny Crosby, she did not let her physical limitations prevent her from leaving us with an incredible legacy of her writing. This is the only known biography of Annie Johnson Flint, who died in 1932, and was first published in 1948 by the Evangelical Press. The story is told by Roland V. Bingham [1872-1942] who was the founder of the Sudan Interior Mission and knew Annie personally. This account of her life, as well as telling her remarkable triumph over severe physical adversity, also records the only known 'autobiography' of hers, together with a selection of her poetry.

Purchase from Amazon.com

Purchase from Amazon.co.uk

He Giveth More Grace: One Hundred Poems by Annie Johnson Flint

This collection of one hundred of her poems contains all of Annie's most well-known writings, as well many of the lesser-known ones. Many of them reflect an unwavering faith in her God and and His promises and a belief that He was always with her and supporting her, and that He had a plan for her life, even though her way might be hard and she couldn't currently see what his purposes for her might be. Her unwavering reliance on God's grace to cope with trials on a daily basis is also very evident, as is her deep love for her Saviour, Jesus Christ. What also shines through many of her poems is a love of God's creation, and this fact is made all the more remarkable because her arthritis would have prevented her from exploring so much of it.

Purchase from Amazon.com

Purchase from Amazon.co.uk

God Hath Not Promised - One Hundred More Poems by Annie Johnson Flint

Ravi Zacharias has described Annie Johnson Flint as the greatest of hymnwriters, and this second of three newly published volumes of her work illustrates why she is held in such high regard by the countless thousands who have enjoyed and have been encouraged by her poems over the last 100 years. Together with her biography, 'The Making of the Beautiful', this collection of Annie's legacy is certain to be enjoyed by a new audience.

Purchase from Amazon.com

Purchase from Amazon.co.uk

MORE FROM HAYDEN PRESS

100 Hymns and Poems of Love and Devotion

This book comprises 100 hymns and poems that each express love and devotion to the Lord Jesus or to God the Father, with contributions from writers such as Charles Wesley, Daniel Webster Whittle, Horatius Bonar, J.N. Darby, C.H. Gabriel, Annie Johnson Flint, P.P. Bliss, Frances Ridley Havergal and Fanny J. Crosby. Also included are biographies of 17 of the authors.

Link to Amazon.com

Link to Amazon.co.uk

The Life and Life-Work of P.P. Bliss - A Biography

P.P. Bliss was one of the most gifted hymnwriters and composers of the late Victorian era, known for hymns such as Man of Sorrows, Dare to be a Daniel, I Will Sing of My Redeemer, Ho! My Comrades, See the Signal, Brightly Beams Our Father's Mercy and More Holiness Give Me. As this biography records, Bliss's life was tragically cut short, but not before he had left a legacy that is a source of joy and encouragement to millions of Christians today.

Link to Amazon.com

Link to Amazon.co.uk

Printed in Great Britain
by Amazon

87765701R00108